Praise for *Simply Speaking!*

Fantastic information for anybody who wants to improve their speaking style or their presentation skills.

Nido Qubein, Past President
National Speakers Association

Simply Speaking! has become the bible we use to ensure that our presenters shine in the spotlight.

Joyce Cox, Director of Training
BellSouth Corporation

Outstanding! My students and I enjoy the layout and the step-by-step formulas. It's one of few books students thoroughly read and retain for future reference.

Sharon Rodriguez, Senior Professor
DeVry Institute of Technology

A terrific framework for developing your message and invaluable techniques for handling the fear!

Denise Hipps, CPA, Director
PriceWaterhouseCoopers

David Greenberg's approach is unique and far better than I have ever encountered.

Scan Putegnat, Business Development Manager
Hitachi Telecom

David Greenberg's books and programs are tremendous. They have been extremely beneficial for our salespeople.

Mark Myette, Director of Training and Sales Development
Dictaphone Corporation

If you want to be a powerful presenter, attend one of David Greenberg's workshops or read this book!

Lynn Thomas, Training Manager
AT&T

DAVID GREENBERG'S

Simply Speaking!

The No-Sweat Way to Prepare and Deliver Presentations

Third Edition

Goldleaf Publications, Atlanta, Georgia

DAVID GREENBERG'S

Simply
Speaking!

The No-Sweat
Way to Prepare and
Deliver Presentations

Third Edition

Library of Congress Catalog Number: 97-91791
ISBN 1-890480-00-2

Printed in the United States of America.
"Simply Speaking" is a trademark of
David Greenberg's Simply Speaking, Inc. ®
Cover design by Ad Graphics, Tulsa, Oklahoma.

You may order additional copies by calling
Toll-free 1-888-773-2512

Published by
Goldleaf Publications, Atlanta, Georgia

Special thanks to Mom and Dad, the members of Buckhead Toastmasters, The National Speakers Association, and my Sixth-grade teacher Mrs. Weir, wherever you are.

This book is dedicated to the memory of Gigi Gabay, who, as President of my Toastmasters club, whispered three words during my first speech which changed my life—"He's a natural." Natural or not, thank you for your encouraging words!

*To do the common thing
uncommonly well brings success.*

John D. Rockefeller

Contents

Four Stages of a Speaker's Development

1. "Anything that can get me through this is good enough."

2. "Hey. It's not bad up here."

3. "It's almost like sitting around the dinner table."

4. "I have something to say!"

From *The Toastmaster Magazine*

Introduction

My first audience was in junior high school—Mrs. Weir's Sixth-grade English class. It was an oral book report. Remember those days? I approached the front of the room, clenched the lectern for support and managed to squeak out five words: "Good afternoon, my name is . . ." I completely froze, forgot my name, and never even started the book report!

Years later I realized the importance of being an effective communicator, and in 1985, I joined a Toastmasters club. During my "Icebreaker" speech, I saw the club President turn to another woman and whisper, "He's a natural!" I felt so proud, even though I knew it was not all natural ability—I had practiced that speech at least twenty times!

That evening I realized that if one learns how to prepare and practice, public speaking could be a wonderfully rewarding experience. Though still nervous, I sought every opportunity to speak. Eventually I won several speaking competitions. Oglethorpe University hired me to teach their presentation skills classes and people from all types of organizations called me to help them improve their communication skills. In 1988, my company, Simply Speaking, Inc.®, was born. A decade later in 1998, the National Speakers Association honored me with their highest-earned award, the Certified Speaking Professional. The "CSP" designation is held by less than 7% of the organization's four thousand members.

Being a powerful communicator has a tremendous transfer value to everything we do. Through my company's workshops, I have witnessed transformations going far beyond improved presentation skills, including increased self-esteem, greater self-confidence and an increased desire to tackle other challenges.

I have personally felt the debilitating fear of public speaking, and I know what it is like to bask in the applause and "great presentation" accolades. That is the feeling I want all my readers and workshop participants to experience. So, read on!

*Never rise to speak 'til you
have something to say;
and when you've said it, cease.*

Calvin Coolidge

Section I
Preparing and Practicing Your Winning Presentation

Top Adult Fears

1. **Speaking Before a Group**

2. Heights

3. Insects and Bugs

4. Financial Problems

5. Deep Water

6. Sickness

7. **Death**

People's Almanac Presents The Book of Lists

Chapter 1
Reducing Speech Anxiety

All speakers have experienced some form of speech anxiety. According to *The Book of Lists,* the number one fear of most people is *speaking before a group!* If you have any anxiety about public speaking, at least you have plenty of company. Notice that fear number seven on that same list is *death!*

The tips in this chapter are designed to help you control your presentation jitters and make those annoying butterflies "fly in formation."

Tips to Reduce Your Anxiety

Tip #1: It's good to be nervous.

Every speaker I know gets nervous before speaking. Being nervous means you care about giving a good presentation. Your nervousness produces adrenaline which helps you think faster, speak more fluently, and add the needed enthusiasm to convey your message.

Tip #2: Don't try to be perfect.

The fear of public speaking often stems from a fear of imperfection. Accept the fact that no one ever gets it perfect and neither will you. You do not have to become *Super Speaker,* never saying "er" or "uh," and never losing your train of thought. Be yourself—your audience will appreciate it.

Tip #3: Visualize your success.

Close your eyes (finish reading this paragraph first) and picture yourself delivering your talk with confidence and enthusiasm. What does the room look like? What do the people look like? How are you standing and moving? Picture your entire presentation in great detail, then read the rest of this book to help turn that picture into a reality!

Tip #4: Know your subject.

Dale Carnegie used to say, "Earn the right" to talk about your subject. Become an authority on your topic. The more you know, the more confident you will be.

Tip #5: Breathe.

Before and even during your presentation, take a few deep breaths. As you inhale, say to yourself, "I am," and as you exhale, "relaxed." Just before your presentation, leave the meeting room and go for a walk. Take some deep breaths and give yourself a pep talk.

Tip #6: Practice, practice, practice!

Question: How do you get to Carnegie Hall?
Answer: Practice! The best way to reduce your anxiety is to rehearse until you feel comfortable. See page 38 for tips on what and how to practice.

Tip #7: The audience wants you to succeed.

Your listeners *want* you to do well. Think of them as your support team—they are on your side.

Tip #8. Make eye contact.

This can work wonders! Not only will the audience appreciate it, but you will *see* that they are interested in your message. Add a smile and you are bound to see some in return. Start with a few friendly faces in different areas of the room.

Tip #9. Involve your audience.

Ask listeners questions or have them participate in an activity. Keeping your audience actively involved will hold their attention, increase their retention, and reduce your nervousness. For other ideas, see *Spicing-Up Your Presentations.*

Tip #10. Focus on your audience and your message.

What you have to say is important! People need to hear your message. Focus on that, rather than on your nervousness. You can do this!

Common Worries and Cures

**"My heart races," "I turn red," or
"I sweat a lot."**
Before you speak, avoid caffeine and alcohol, eat a
small meal, and *over-prepare* the first few minutes
of your presentation—this is typically the most
nerve-wracking time.

"I speak too fast."
Increase your eye contact. When you look into people's eyes, it's
difficult to talk at a rate faster than they can easily understand.
Also, pause and silently count "one-two" after important ideas so
listeners can digest what you've said. For more tips, see pages 96
and 97.

"My mouth goes dry."
Keep a *room-temperature* glass of water nearby. Pause and sip
some water after important points.

"I'm afraid I'll go blank."
To prevent it, *over-prepare* and practice speaking from *useful*
notes (see page 35). To recover if it happens, pause and look at
your notes. Although it may seem like an eternity *to you*, this will
take only a few seconds. If you're still clueless, ask the audience,
"Where was I?" They are typically eager to help.

"I tend to ramble or go off on a tangent."
Practice speaking from *useful* notes (see page 35) and
sticking to the agenda. Before you make a point, ask
yourself, "Do they really *need* to know this?" If not,
skip it. Listeners can ask questions if they desire
additional information.

18

"I'm afraid I'll be boring" or "I can't tell jokes."
You don't have to tell jokes to be interesting. Read Section II,
Spicing-Up Your Presentations.

**"I'm afraid someone will ask a question I
can't answer."**
You're not expected to know everything. Read Chapter
4, *Mastering Question-and-Answer Sessions.*

"My accent or dialect may be hard to understand."
Ask your friends and colleagues for honest feedback as to whether
your accent interferes with your communication. It may be
working *for* you—consider Arnold Schwarzenegger. Aside from
seeking help from an accent reduction specialist, slow down your
rate of speech, repeat important ideas and pause frequently to
allow listeners time to absorb your points. See page 97 for
additional tips.

"I say *um* and *ah* too much."
Most of us use these "fillers" occasionally while formulating our
thoughts. Used too often, they can be very annoying to listeners.
To reduce them, first, try to catch the start of *um* and *ah* (you can
feel it formulating in your vocal cords), then replace it with a
pause. Count silently "one-two." This takes practice, but will be
much appreciated by listeners. See page 97 for additional tips.

"I don't like to make eye contact."
During your practice sessions, ask members of your audience to
raise their hand when they feel you have made *sufficient* eye
contact with them. Your goal is to get everyone to have a hand
raised. Review the additional tips on page 96.

"I don't know what to do with my hands."
Your gestures should underscore your spoken message. Review the
many tips on page 95 for gesturing effectively.

If you can't get people to listen to you any other way, tell them it's confidential.

The Farmer's Digest

Chapter 2
Preparing Your Presentation
Step-by-Step

Step #1. Understand your audience

Step #2. Establish your objectives

Step #3. Brainstorm ideas

Step #4. Play solitaire to organize

Step #5. Create your conclusion

Step #6. Create your opening

Step #7. Reduce your content

Step #8. Create useful notes

Step #9. Practice everything

There is no substitute for preparation. It is the best way to reduce any speech anxiety and ensure that your presentation is a success. This chapter will show you, step-by-step, how to prepare and rehearse a well-organized presentation that gets your message across clearly, concisely, and convincingly.

The "Three Tell 'Ems"

To be effective, your presentation must be well organized and easy to follow. Most presentations have a three-part structure containing an *opening*, a *body* and a *conclusion*. We will refer to this structure as the "Three Tell 'Ems." In the opening, *tell 'em what you're gonna' tell 'em.* In the body, *tell 'em.* And in the conclusion, *tell 'em what you've told 'em.*

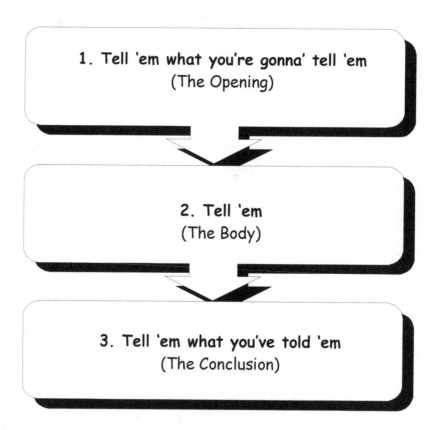

1. Tell 'em what you're gonna' tell 'em
(The Opening)

2. Tell 'em
(The Body)

3. Tell 'em what you've told 'em
(The Conclusion)

Step #1:
Understand Your Audience

There is a story of a young woman standing on a bridge, preparing to plunge into the depths of the river below. A psychologist, a police officer, and a pastor pleaded with her, giving her all their reasons to go on living, but to no avail. Suddenly another young woman observing this hopeless situation shouted, "You don't want to jump into that stinkin' dirty water. It's filthy!" The would-be suicide victim promptly climbed down from the bridge.

In order to influence others to listen to your ideas, you must touch what is important to *them*. As the expression goes, "Before I can sell what Jane Jones buys, I must see through Jane Jones' eyes." Use the Audience Analysis Worksheet on the next page to gain an understanding of your listeners. If you need assistance, contact the person who invited you to speak, other speakers who have addressed this group or some members of the audience.

Audience Analysis Worksheet — The Five "W's"

WHO?
Name of group: _____ Number attending?____ Mandatory or voluntary? % male/female:___ Spouses/partners attending? Y N Occupations: _____ Average age: ____ Average income: ____ Education: _____

WHY?
Why is the group meeting? _____ Why did they invite me to speak? _____

WHAT?
What is important to this group? _____ What are some of this group's strengths? _____ What are some of their biggest challenges? _____ What does this group need to learn? _____ What concerns or objections might they have? _____ What special needs might they have? _____ What motivates them?_____ What turns them off? _____ What is their general attitude about my topic? _____

WHERE?
Location: _____ Phone: _____ Room: _____ Configuration: _____

WHEN?
Date: _____ Start Time: _____ End Time: _____ What's on the agenda before and after me? _____

Step #2:
Establish Your Objectives

What is the purpose of your presentation? What do you want listeners to know, feel, or do? To help you focus your purpose and determine the necessary content for your presentation, write down your objective(s) using one simple *purpose statement*. To do this, picture yourself standing before your audience, saying a phrase such as one of the following:

"My purpose today is to . . .

- Reveal the secrets of . . ."
- Unravel the mystery behind . . ."
- Prove to you . . ."
- Show you the three advantages of . . ."
- Provide you the four key ingredients for . . ."
- Share with you what it's like to . . ."
- Introduce you to . . ."
- Help you understand . . ."
- Give you a guided tour of . . ."
- Share with you three proven strategies for . . ."
- Tell you what few people know about . . ."
- Teach you the one tool that will help you . . ."

In this chapter, we will prepare a sample presentation with the following purpose statement:

My purpose today is to show you the advantages of replacing our accounting software.

✎ Your turn. Write down your purpose statement:

_____

_____

_____

Know that your listeners will be tuned-in to the most popular "station" in the world, "WII-FM." The letters stand for *What's In It For Me?* In other words, why should your audience care about your message? If this is not clear from your purpose statement, either revise it or add a *benefit statement* such as, "This will be important to you because . . ."

For our sample presentation, we might say:

This will be important to you because the new software can make your jobs easier and less stressful.

✎ Your turn. Based on your audience analysis, why is it important for listeners to pay attention to you?

_____

_____

_____

Step #3:
Brainstorm Ideas

How can you achieve your presentation objectives? What do your listeners need to know? Using sticky notes or pieces of scrap paper, brainstorm possible ideas. To help generate ideas, you may wish to refer to own your personal experiences, friends, audience members, industry experts, clients and customers, library reference desks, trade publications, company literature, schools, newspapers, magazines, television, radio, or the Internet.

Carry sticky notes and a manila folder with you everywhere, even at your bedside. Anytime an idea pops into mind, jot it down and put it in your folder. Write only *one* idea per sticky note, and generate more ideas than you will need for your talk—you will edit later. For now, if an idea has any possible merit, write it down, put the paper in a manila folder, and move to your next idea (see example on next page).

After brainstorming ideas for several minutes, here are several of the benefits of the new accounting software we may wish to include in our sample presentation:

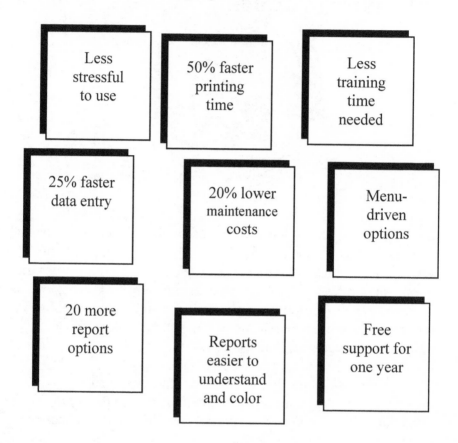

Step #4:
Play Solitaire to Organize the Body of Your Presentation

Similar to playing solitaire with a deck of cards, arrange your ideas into columns of *related* ideas. Ideally, you should have no more than three to five columns. Try various arrangements until you discover one you feel works best. When you find an arrangement you like, write down the *main idea* for each column, with the related supporting ideas below (see example on next page). These columns of ideas form the *body* of your presentation.

Place your most important column first, followed by the second most important column, and so on. Within each column, arrange the ideas in descending order of importance (your most important ideas on top).

After a few rounds of "solitaire," this is one of many possible arrangements for the body of our sample presentation.

Main Ideas:

#1 EASIER TO USE	#2 BETTER REPORTS	#3 SAVES MONEY

Related Supporting Ideas:

Less stressful to use	20 more report options	Less training time needed
25% faster data entry	50% faster printing time	20% lower maintenance costs
Menu-driven options	Reports easier to understand and color	Free support for one year

Step #5:
Tell 'Em What You've Told 'Em
(Create Your Conclusion)

An effective conclusion provides listeners with a sense of closure and answers the question, "Now what?" Your conclusion is the last thing your audience will hear from you and possibly what they will remember best. Plan this section carefully and be sure to accomplish the following:

1. Signal that you are nearing the end.
When an audience hears words such as "In conclusion . . ." or "To summarize . . ." they typically listen more carefully.

2. Review or summarize the main ideas.
Briefly restate your three to five main ideas. Use a phrase such as "Here are the three main ideas to remember . . ."

3. End with a bang, not a whimper.
End in a memorable way. What do you want your listeners to do now that they have heard your presentation? Consider ending with a recommendation, a challenge, a prediction or a simple parting thought or quotation. Make sure your closing words are concise and, if calling for action, specific. Use a phrase such as "I leave you with this thought . . ." or "I urge you to . . ."

Step #6:
Tell 'Em What You're Gonna'
Tell 'Em (Create Your Opening)

You have only a few seconds to convince listeners that you have something important to say. Plan this section carefully and be sure to accomplish the following:

1. Start with a compelling Attention-Getter.

Start with a powerful story or one of the other "Attention Getters" on the next page to pull listeners into your presentation and help them focus on you and your message.

2. State your purpose and tune-in to WII-FM?

Review your *purpose statement* on page 26 and tell listeners what you plan to achieve. Answer their question, "What's in it for me (the listener)?" Use phrases such as "My purpose today is to . . ." and "This will be important to you because . . ."

3. Provide a preview or "road map."

Explain how you have organized your presentation and how many points you will discuss. Use a phrase such as "Here are the three main points I will discuss: First I will discuss [main idea #1], second [main idea #2], and third [main idea #3]."

Effective Attention-Getters

Stories (see Chapter 9, *Using Humor and Stories*)
Look for stories that illustrate your points. Begin with a phrase like, "Let me tell you a story about . . ." or just *relive* the story with the audience, "It started like any other day, when suddenly . . ." Then show how the story illustrates your speech purpose or point.

Intriguing questions
"What would you do with one extra hour each month?" Pause and raise your hand if you want responses.

Startling facts or statistics
"One out of five people in this room will die of heart disease! Look at four people sitting near you. How do you fare?"

Quotations
"Gypsy Rose Lee once said, 'Anything worth doing is worth doing slowly.' I believe we can improve our product's quality by slowing down our assembly process and paying closer attention to detail."

Challenging statements
"If your company doesn't have a website, you'll be out of business within three years. Today, I will show you how to develop a website that will help grow your business."

News items
"*Investors Daily News* states that twenty percent of Fortune 100 companies will *not* be in that category in five years! Today, I will show you how we can secure our position."

Eye-catching props
"This $25 book can save our company millions of dollars!"

Step #7:
Reduce Your Content

When I went backpacking for the first time, a friend advised me, "Pack everything you *think* you will need. Then unpack and repack only *half* of the items. Your pack will be lighter and you will enjoy the trip more." It is now time for you to "unpack" and repack about 50 to 75 percent of your original presentation content. It's better to clearly convey a few points than to race through and overwhelm listeners with a "data dump." Review your audience analysis and your presentation objectives, then eliminate ideas that may:

- Overwhelm listeners

- Weaken the strength of other ideas

- Be presented during the Q&A session, if necessary

- Be included in a detailed handout, but not discussed

- Be saved for a follow-up presentation

- Make the presentation too long

Step #8:
Create Useful Notes

Useful notes are LARGE, easy-to-read, and well-organized key words and symbols that jog your memory and help you discuss your ideas *conversationally*. They may also contain sketches of graphics you will draw during your talk, questions you will ask, and delivery reminders like "Make eye contact!" In most cases, useful notes are *not* a script containing every word you plan to say. Chances are you will either read or memorize a script and risk boring your audience to tears.

If you have followed the steps in this chapter, the sticky notes you organized in your manila folder may serve as useful notes from which you can speak. You may prefer to copy the ideas on your sticky notes onto a larger piece of paper in the form of an outline (see example on next page). When I used to perform stand-up comedy, I would write my notes on the palm of my hand. I learned the hard way that this is not a good idea if you tend to sweat.

Sample Outline and Notes

The Opening (memorized, not read)

"What would you do with an extra hour or two every month? You are wasting at least that much time using our outdated accounting software. My purpose today is to show you the advantages of replacing our accounting software. This will be important to you because the new software I have researched can make your jobs easier and less stressful. First, I'll demonstrate how easy the new software is to use. Second, I'll show you its powerful reports. And third, I'll focus on the tremendous cost savings."

The Body (useful notes to jog your memory)

1. EASY TO USE
    - Stress ⬇
    - 25% faster data entry
    - Menu-driven options

2. POWERFUL REPORTS
    - 20 more reports
    - 50% faster printing time
    - Easier to understand/color

3. SAVES $$$
    - Training needed ⬇
    - 20% lower maint. cost
    - Free support 1 year

The Conclusion (memorized, not read)

"In conclusion, the key points to remember are: First, the new system is easier to use; second, it provides much better reports; and third, it saves us a lot of money. I urge you to approve this purchase."

The Three Tell 'Ems Outline

The Opening: Tell 'em what you're gonna tell 'em
1. Start with a compelling Attention-Getter.
2. State your purpose and tune-in to WII-FM?
3. Provide a preview or road map.

The Body: Tell 'em
1. Main Idea #1
    Supporting evidence, proof, statistics, facts, testimonies, quotes, anecdotes, demonstrations, examples, personal stories, etc.
    Transition to next point.
2. Main Idea #2
    Supporting evidence, proof, statistics, facts, testimonies, quotes, anecdotes, demonstrations, examples, personal stories, etc.
    Transition to next point.
3. Main Idea #3
    Supporting evidence, proof, statistics, facts, testimonies, quotes, anecdotes, demonstrations, examples, personal stories, etc.
    Transition to conclusion.

The Conclusion: Tell 'em what you've told 'em
1. Signal that you are nearing the end.
2. Review or summarize the main ideas.
3. Provide a call for action or a parting thought

Step #9:
Practice Everything!

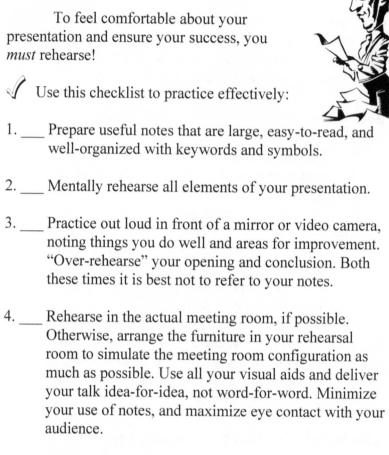

To feel comfortable about your presentation and ensure your success, you *must* rehearse!

✓ Use this checklist to practice effectively:

1. ___ Prepare useful notes that are large, easy-to-read, and well-organized with keywords and symbols.

2. ___ Mentally rehearse all elements of your presentation.

3. ___ Practice out loud in front of a mirror or video camera, noting things you do well and areas for improvement. "Over-rehearse" your opening and conclusion. Both these times it is best not to refer to your notes.

4. ___ Rehearse in the actual meeting room, if possible. Otherwise, arrange the furniture in your rehearsal room to simulate the meeting room configuration as much as possible. Use all your visual aids and deliver your talk idea-for-idea, not word-for-word. Minimize your use of notes, and maximize eye contact with your audience.

5. ___ Ask your friends, family or colleagues to critique your practice sessions (use the Presentation Feedback Form on the next page) and incorporate any changes that will make your presentation more effective.

6. ___ Practice with the presentation in its final form, noting any time constraints.

Presentation Feedback Form

The Opening

Appearance: _____

Compelling Attention-Getter: _____

Purpose Statement/WII-FM: _____

Preview/Road map: _____

The Body

Organization: _____

Clarity: _____

Transitions: _____

Persuasiveness: _____

The Conclusion

Summary: _____

Call for action: _____

The Delivery

Attitude: _____

Body language: _____

Voice: _____

Word choice: _____

Interaction with audience: _____

Visual aids: _____

Presentation Preparation Checklist

✓ To prepare my presentation, I have:

1. ___ analyzed my audience and their needs

2. ___ established my objective(s) and written a clear purpose statement and benefit statement, if necessary

3. ___ brainstormed ideas to achieve my objective(s)

4. ___ played solitaire to organize my ideas

5. ___ created a conclusion where I:

   ___ signaled that I am nearing the end

   ___ briefly reviewed or summarized my main ideas

   ___ provided a call for action or a parting thought

6. ___ created an opening where I:

   ___ started with a compelling Attention-Getter

   ___ stated my objectives and tuned-in to "WII-FM?"

   ___ provided a preview or road map introducing the main points

7. ___ reduced my content to what listeners *need* to know

8. ___ created useful notes (not a script in most cases)

9. ___ practiced everything out loud, received feedback and made any necessary changes

Chapter 3
Preparing Winning
Team Presentations

When conducted effectively, team presentations can be exciting and dynamic, keeping listeners attentive. The key to a successful team presentation is solid planning and preparation. Without it, your presentation can seem disjointed and unprofessional. This chapter will help you overcome some of the common pitfalls of team presentations and ensure that your team shines in the spotlight.

TIP: Visit large trade shows and learn from some true masters of team presentations. Often you'll see team-style presentations from major corporations. These companies have invested a lot of time and money to develop presentations that are both entertaining and informative.

Team Presentation Checklist

✓ To ensure your team presentation is successful:

1. ____ Pick a strong team leader.

2. ____ Ensure that each team member is committed to making the other team members look great and that there are no hidden agendas to "steal the show."

3. ____ Analyze your audience (review Step #1 from Chapter Two for help).

4. ____ Establish your objectives (review Step #2 from Chapter Two for help).

5. ____ Brainstorm content ideas (review Step #3 from Chapter Two for help). Give each team member a marker and a pad of large sticky notes. Post the ideas on the meeting room wall so everyone can see them and participate in the brainstorming.

6. ____ Play solitaire to organize ideas into columns of related ideas (review Step #4 from Chapter Two for help).

7. ____ Consider each team member's strengths and decide who will cover which points and answer specific questions.

8. ____ Select appropriate team-teaching approaches. Try using more than one approach for the sake of variety and interest.

9. Assign responsibilities for:
___ Preparing/delivering standardized speaker introductions
___ Creating standardized visual aids and handouts
___ Scheduling rehearsal times and locations
___ Timing each presenter and providing cues ("1 min. left")
___ Taking charge of the presentation environment and
audio-visual needs

10. ___ At this time, you may need to work individually or in sub-groups to further develop the presentation. Agree on times allotted for each portion and when you will reconvene.

11. ___ Practice *everything* out loud, including a full rehearsal no more than two days before the presentation. Decide where the team members will stand when they are *not* speaking (Note: Look at the person who is speaking and look interested).

12. ___ Arrive at the meeting room *at least* one hour early to ensure everything is as needed, practice a last time if necessary, and greet your listeners.

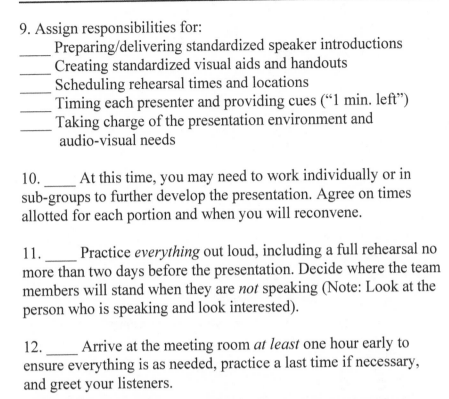

TIP: The most common team approach is where one person welcomes the audience, kicks off the presentation, introduces the players, then each presenter speaks for an allotted time. The same member who kicked off the presentation facilitates a Q&A session, summarizes the main ideas, and closes the show. This format can work well. However, if there are several presenters, it may not be the most interesting format. Consider incorporating other formats, such as a game show format, a "point-counterpoint" segment, a planted "heckler" in the audience posing challenging scenarios, a "tag-team" approach similar to a wrestling match, or a television-style commercial involving the entire team. Be creative and have fun. Your audience will appreciate it.

Does anyone have any questions for my answers?

Henry Kissinger

Chapter 4
Mastering
Question-and-Answer Sessions

The question-and-answer session, or "Q&A," often is the most important part of a presentation. It allows listeners to have their specific concerns addressed, enables you to ensure that they understand your message, and allows you to tie up any loose ends. The tips in this chapter will help you prepare for and conduct an effective Q&A session.

Typically, the Q&A is held near the end of the presentation, after a review or summary of the main ideas. This reminds listeners what was discussed in order to formulate questions. In the beginning of your presentation, you may wish to tell listeners when and how you will handle their questions. Use a phrase like "I will be glad to answer any questions at the end of the program. If something is unclear, please feel free to ask at anytime."

Starting Your Q&A Session

Tip #1. Act as if you really want questions.

Merely asking "Are there any questions?" often gets blank stares from audience members and the Q&A session falls flat. To let listeners know you want questions:
- Step forward to connect with the audience
- Ask enthusiastically, *"What* questions can I answer for you?"
- Pause for a few seconds to encourage a response
- Raise your own hand if you want others to do so

Tip #2. "Plant" questions.

If you think the audience may be reluctant to ask questions, solicit a few people beforehand to prepare a question or tell them a question you would like them to ask.

Tip #3. Ask your own questions.

If no one asks a question, you may need to get things rolling. You might say, "A question I am often asked is . . ." or "Something I barely touched on is . . ." This typically prompts other questions. In addition, you could use this technique to cover topics that you left out of the body of your presentation.

Tip #4. Ask listeners to put questions in writing.

With very large groups or for times when you want control over the questions you are asked, request that listeners write down their questions on cards and pass them to you. As a result, you can answer (or not answer) the questions in the order *you* desire. You can even add your own questions to the pile without listeners being aware that they are your questions.

Answering Questions

Tip #1. Anticipate potential questions.
Practice your talk in front of colleagues, friends, or perhaps people from the group you will address. Encourage them to ask tough questions. If you are able to answer their questions, you are probably ready to face your "real" audience.

Tip #2. Repeat or summarize the question.
If there is a chance someone did not hear the question, repeat it. Also, if you are asked a complicated question, rephrase it so both you and the audience understand the question (this will also provide you a little added time to formulate your answer).

Tip #3. Do not bluff or panic.

If you cannot adequately answer a question, ask the audience for possible answers or say, "I will research that and get you an answer by . . ." Ask the person who raised the question to write it on the back of a business card and give it to you after the presentation as a reminder.

Ending Your Q&A Session
After you answer the last question, restate your main points, then call for action or leave listeners with your parting thought. Say something like, "We are almost out of time. I will be glad to stay and answer any additional questions or feel free to call me. To summarize, the three reasons to approve this project are [point 1], [point 2], and [point 3]. If you want to be more effective, I urge you to adopt my proposal."

Q&A Session Worksheet

Be prepared! Jot down questions your listeners might ask you and questions you might ask to get your Q&A session started, if necessary. Naturally, develop answers to these questions.

1. _____

_____

_____

2. _____

_____

_____

3. _____

_____

_____

4. _____

_____

_____

5. _____

_____

_____

Q&A Session Checklist

✓ To start my Q&A session, I will:

1. ___ act as if I really want questions

2. ___ plant questions

3. ___ ask my own questions, if necessary

4. ___ ask listeners to put questions in writing, if appropriate

✓ To answer questions effectively, I will:

1. ___ anticipate potential questions

2. ___ repeat or summarize questions

3. ___ not bluff or panic

✓ To end my Q&A session, I will:

1. ___ tell listeners I am available after the program to answer additional questions

2. ___ briefly restate my main points

3. ___ call for action and/or state my parting thought

Eighty percent of success is showing up.

Woody Allen

Don't leave the remaining twenty percent to chance.

David Greenberg

Chapter 5
Taking Charge of Your Presentation Environment

After spending hours preparing your presentation, do not leave the details of your speaking environment to chance! Too many speakers' messages have been lost or weakened because their audiences were uncomfortable or distracted by the speaking environment. As the speaker, you should be in control of *everything* which can affect your presentation.

Call the meeting planner and specify your needs. Arrive at least an hour early to familiarize yourself with your speaking environment, practice a last time and ensure everything is the way you want. This chapter will discuss some of the major elements of your speaking environment and provide a detailed checklist to ensure all the "little" things are handled.

Microphones ("Mikes")

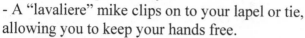

- Use mikes with groups larger than about 25 people or if you tend to speak softly.
- A "lavaliere" mike clips on to your lapel or tie, allowing you to keep your hands free.
- Request a cordless mike or ample cord so you can walk around freely.
- Perform a sound-check well *before* your audience arrives so you don't have to ask the audience "Is this on?" or "Can you hear me?"

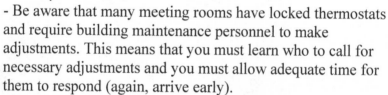

Lighting

- The more light, the more alert the group—keep 'em bright.
- Arrive early and learn how to operate the lighting controls—some controls can be complicated (ask for help).
- If the lights directly over your screen are too bright and cannot be dimmed, unscrew bulbs (ask for help).

Room Temperature

- Be aware that many meeting rooms have locked thermostats and require building maintenance personnel to make adjustments. This means that you must learn who to call for necessary adjustments and you must allow adequate time for them to respond (again, arrive early).
- It's typically best to set the room cooler than normal. It will warm from the body heat of the audience.

Lecterns, Stages, and Risers

- Request a lectern (often mistakenly called a "podium") to hold your notes. Place it to one side of the center of the stage area, allowing you to stand center stage *without* standing (hiding) behind it. Angle it so you can easily see your notes.
- If speaking to more than about 30 people, request a stage/riser to stand on so people can see you more easily.

Seating Configurations

Conference Tables
- Fosters team spirit for up to about a dozen people.
- Stand at the head of the table to gain attention and enhance your position as an authority.

U-Shape/Semi-Circle
- Positions you as an authority when you stand in front.
- Because participants can see each other, the configuration encourages group interaction.
- Ample room for you to move in the middle of the "U" and walk up close to each participant.
- Visual aids are easily displayed and seen.

Circle Seating
- Because participants can see each other, the configuration encourages group interaction.
- You can join the circle and position yourself as a peer.
- You can stand outside the circle to separate yourself from the group and allow participants to work without your influence.
- Usually good for groups smaller than twenty-five.
- Can be awkward if participants do not know or like each other. Consider opening with an "ice-breaker" activity.

Theater or Classroom Seating
- Enhances your position as an authority/instructor.
- Learn from the theater—use two side aisles rather than a center aisle, and angle the side sections toward the stage ("chevron" style). Angled rows allow participants to see others in their own row and increase comfort, laughter and learning. Straight rows bleed energy from a group.
- Remove or rope-off extra chairs before participants arrive.

Speaking Environment Planner

Meeting Date: _____ Start Time: _____ End Time: _____
Location: _____ Room Number/Name: _____
Facility Coordinator: _____ Phone: _____
Early access for practicing your presentation, hours: _____

Seating Configuration

___ Conference	___ Semi-Circle	___ Classroom
___ U-Shape	___ Circle	___ Theater

Materials Needed

Qty.	Qty.	Qty.
___ Tables	___ Overhead projector	___ Monitor
___ Chairs	___ Data projector	___ Screen
___ Podium	___ Slide projector	___ Video camera
___ Microphone	___ Flip charts	___ Pads/pencils
___ Extension cord	___ Pointer	___ Refreshments
___ Stage/riser	___ VCR/DVD player	___ Other _____

Arrive at least one hour early and check the following:

___ Back rows taped or roped off
___ Temperature comfortable
___ Lighting adjusted correctly
___ Location of lighting and climate controls
___ Effective lectern position and staging
___ Tested and know how to operate all necessary audio-visual equipment
___ Tested visual aids for visibility from all areas of room
___ Projector lenses cleaned and focused
___ Spare bulbs and backup equipment readily available
___ Projector table has space for transparencies and notes
___ Ample flip chart paper, fresh markers, tape, and push pins
___ Microphone has a fresh battery and replacement available
___ Microphone tested for volume level and feedback spots
___ Handouts distributed

Chapter 6
Handling Difficult Situations
and Audience Members

Do not let a difficult or possibly hostile audience come as a last minute surprise. If appropriate, ask the person who invited you about the audience's opinion of you and your topic, as well as any hidden agendas and the names of any especially troublesome participants. This advanced knowledge, along with the tips in this chapter, will help you prepare for and avoid the pitfalls of an otherwise difficult situation.

Handling Difficult Situations

When your topic is controversial:

Tip #1. Start with your least controversial topics. Find a common ground on which everyone can agree; then work your way toward the more controversial areas.

Tip #2. Empathize—show listeners that you understand their feelings, even if you do not agree with them. Say something like, "I understand how you could feel [feeling] . . ."

Tip #3. Remind listeners of your common ground if things get rough, and once again when calling for action.

When your meeting heads in the "wrong" direction:

Tip #1. If someone raises an issue you would rather not discuss, you might say, "That's beyond the scope of our program. May I get with you later?"

Tip #2. Be sure each participant has a meeting agenda and say, "Let's keep to the agenda, and I will add your item to our next meeting's agenda."

Tip #3. Write the words "Parking Lot" on a flip chart page. Post it on the *back* wall, write down the issue and say, "I'm temporarily parking the issue. It is important. This will remind me to address it later. For now, let's park it and move on."

Tip #4. If your group is unable to move ahead until the issue is discussed, you could say something like, "Let's take fifteen minutes to discuss this, then we will need to move on."

Handling Difficult People

The "Devil's Advocate"

Tip #1. Do not answer a negatively-loaded question until you change it to a neutral question. For example, change "Why do you charge such an excessive amount?" to "Let me explain how we determine our rate structure."

Tip #2. Empathize—show questioners that you understand their feelings, even if you do not agree with them. If someone says, "This is the craziest idea I've heard in a long time," you could say, "I understand how it might seem crazy. Let's see if I can show you how well this can work . . ."

Tip #3. This person can help in some situations, but if you and other meeting participants cannot get your messages across without being interrupted with negativity, ask the entire group to agree to refrain from evaluating ideas until a set time on the agenda.

The "Long-Winded" Participant

Tip #1. Politely interrupt and say something like, "Let me see if I understand your question/comment." Summarize the speaker's words and respond appropriately.

Tip #2. Ask listeners to put their questions in writing and pass them to you. This helps them to ask more concise questions, and allows you to rephrase them as you see fit.

Tip #3. If appropriate, state that because of time constraints, questions and comments will be limited to two minutes each. Have an assistant sound a chime when time has expired.

The "I Can't Stay" Participant

Tip #1. In the beginning of the meeting, ask if anybody must leave early. Peer pressure will usually cause people to commit to staying for the duration.

Tip #2. Ask the person who must leave early to sit nearest the exit to avoid disrupting the meeting when he or she leaves.

Tip #3. If people frequently leave your meetings early, ask participants if your meetings are too long or boring, and adjust as needed.

The Chronic Latecomer

Tip #1. Do not confront this person in front of the group—it may be attention this person craves.

Tip #2. Rather than stopping the meeting to review for this person, politely ask him or her to have a seat and try to catch up. If this person is critical to your meeting and you must review, take a break and do so while allowing the others to leave.

Tip #3. After the meeting, ask the person why he or she is frequently late. Perhaps there is a legitimate excuse or a better time for your meetings.

Tip #4. Be sure that you start your meetings on time. If you do not, do not expect people to come to your meetings on time.

The "Multi-Tasker"

Some participants seem to always tend to other matters while they are in your meeting—their pagers goes off, they receive phone calls, somebody comes to get them, they work on other things or they simply leave to tend to some matter. This can be a distraction to the other participants and certainly makes it difficult for you to get your message across to this person(s).

Tip #1. Stress the importance of your meeting and politely ask this person to hold all calls and other interruptions. (Ask the entire group to put phones and pagers on "vibrate" mode.)

Tip #2. If this person is critical to your meeting, hold the meeting at a time this person is not likely to be interrupted, such as before or after normal work hours, or hold it away from the office where the person is less accessible to others.

Tip #3. Meet with this person separately from the group.

The "Whisperers"

Tip #1. Focus your eye contact and your voice on the culprits to alert them that this behavior is not appreciated, but do not embarrass them—they may be discussing your topic.

Tip #2. Ask the *entire group* if there is a question you can answer or something that needs discussion.

Tip #3. If the whispering persists, tell them when you will be taking a break and ask them to focus their attention on the meeting until the break or politely ask them to step outside the meeting room for their private discussion.

The "Monopolizer"

This person typically wants attention and will do almost anything to get it—do not let him or her steal *your* show.

Tip #1. If answering this person's question, do not ask, "Does that answer your question?" It probably won't. Move on!

Tip #2. You could say, "Thank you for your input. Let's hear from some other people. Who else has an idea?"

Tip #3. Give the attention-grabber a role such as helping you capture ideas on a flip chart. He would probably love the attention.

Tip #4. Take a break and explain the problem to this person.

The "Nap-Time!" Participant

This behavior can be very disruptive to an otherwise energized group (especially if they snore!)

Tip #1. Could you liven things up a bit or does the group need a break? Ask them if you're not sure.

Tip #2. Focus your eye contact and your voice on this person to alert him or her that this behavior is not appreciated.

Tip #2. Find a way to involve this person. You may want to ask for his or her opinion about the current topic, but be careful not to embarrass this person (there may be a valid reason).

Tip #3. Take a break and ask this person the cause of the behavior. If the behavior is not going to change, it might be best to ask him or her to skip the meeting.

Dealing with Difficulties Worksheet

1. What possible difficult speaking situation(s) might you encounter and what strategies will you use to ensure the success of your presentation?

_____

_____

_____

_____

2. Who are possible difficult audience members? What difficulty might they cause? What strategies will you use to ensure the success of your presentation?

_____

_____

_____

_____

The Bottom Line — Take Charge!

You are in-charge of your presentation and viewed by your listeners as being responsible for the meeting environment. You must maintain control in order to keep the respect and attention of your listeners.

*People will accept your idea much
more readily if you tell them
Benjamin Franklin said it first.*

David H. Comins

Chapter 7
Adapting to Listeners' Behavioral Styles

Each of us has a distinct *behavioral style* (sometimes called a "personality type") which determines how we think, feel, and act. If we fail to consider our listeners' styles when delivering our presentations, the benefits of our ideas may fall on deaf ears. But when we adapt to our listeners' styles, we increase their comfort, their willingness to listen, and the likelihood of them accepting our ideas and buying what we are selling (we're all in sales).

This area of study is both fascinating and complex. This chapter will provide you a brief overview of the four behavioral styles so you can learn to recognize them and adapt your presentations accordingly.

Understanding Behavioral Styles

The four behavioral styles are known by many names. To keep things simple, remember the acronym "DISC," which stands for "Dominant," "Interactive," "Steady," and "Conscientious." To illustrate the different styles, we'll look at characters from the television shows *I Love Lucy* and *Cheers*, as well as the cartoon *Peanuts*.

It's important to note that everyone has some degree of *each* of the four styles, and we typically use the style we believe will best meet our needs in our environment. By understanding the needs of each style and learning how to adapt our presentations, conflicts can be greatly reduced and communication can be greatly enhanced.

The Dominant Style
- Sometimes known as "Director" or "Driver."
- Characteristics: adventurous, competitive, decisive, dominating, direct, risk-taking, and results-oriented.
- Motivated by: challenge, control, results, and prestige.
- Fears: losing control and being taken advantage of.
- Examples: *I Love Lucy:* Ricky; *Cheers:* Carla; *Peanuts:* Lucy.

Things you should do: Be clear, specific and to the point. Stick to business and provide options. Know your stuff and be prepared to handle tough objections. Present facts logically and efficiently.

Things you should *not* do: Don't waste their time by being unprepared, trying to build personal relationships, asking lots of rhetorical questions or making chitchat. Don't appear uncertain or disorganized.

The Interactive Style

- Sometimes known as "Expressive," or "Socializer."
- Characteristics: charming, confident, convincing, enthusiastic, inspiring, optimistic, people-oriented, popular, sociable, and trusting.
- Motivated by: freedom of expression, freedom from details, people involvement, public recognition, and relationships.
- Fears: rejection and loss of approval.
- Examples: *I Love Lucy:* Lucy; *Cheers:* Sam; *Peanuts:* Peppermint Patty.

✓ Things you should do: Allow time for relating and socializing. Present in a fun, stimulating, and fast-paced manner. Ask for their opinion. Provide testimonials from people they respect. Put details in writing.

✗ Things you should *not* do: Don't be too "stuffy." Don't overwhelm them with lots of facts, figures and alternatives.

The Steady Style

- Sometimes known as "Amiable" or "Feeler."
- Characteristics: easy going, patient, predictable, relaxed, reliable, sincere, steady, team-oriented, and traditional.
- Motivated by: long-term relationships, maintaining the status-quo, minimizing conflicts, security, and stability.
- Fears: conflict and unpredictability.
- Examples: *I Love Lucy:* Ethel; *Cheers:* Woody; *Peanuts:* Charlie Brown.

✓ Things you should do: Show sincere interest in them as people. Present your case patiently, logically, and step-by-step. Provide assurance of stability. If a decision or action is required, allow them time to process your ideas.

✗ Things you should *not* do: Don't "stick to business." Don't force quick decisions. Don't appear too "slick."

The Conscientious Style

- Sometimes known as "Analytical," or "Cautious."
- Characteristics: accurate, analytical, cautious, conscientious, courteous, detail-oriented, factual, perfectionist, problem-solver, precise, private, and restrained.
- Motivated by: accuracy, maintaining standards, order, and quality.
- Fears: poor quality and criticism of their performance.
- Examples: *I Love Lucy:* Fred; *Cheers:* Lilith; *Peanuts:* Schroeder.

Things you should do: Be prepared and well organized. Use a business-like style. Use logic and provide proof. Develop an "Action Plan" with specific dates and milestones. Allow them time to process your ideas, but be persistent. Provide all the information they need to make a well-informed decision.

Things you should *not* do: Don't be casual, informal or personal. Don't be vague about expectations. Don't force a quick decision.

An intellectual is a person who takes more words than is necessary to tell more than he knows.

Dwight D. Eisenhower

"DISC" Analysis Worksheet

After identifying the behavioral style of the key person(s) to whom you will be presenting, answer the following questions:

Behavioral style(s) of the audience: _____

Given this audience's style(s), during your presentation . . .

1. What are some things you should do?

2. What are some things you should avoid doing?

3. What are some statements you can present that will motivate this audience?

4. What are some fears, objections or concerns this audience may have and how can you address them?

When the congregation falls asleep, there is only one thing to do; provide the usher with a sharp stick and have him prod the preacher.

Henry Ward Beechen

Section II
Spicing-Up
Your Presentations

*When your work speaks for itself,
don't interrupt.*

Henry J. Kaiser

Chapter 8
Creating and Using Visual Aids

In our *Simply Speaking!*® workshops, I often mention one of my favorite *I Love Lucy* episodes, where Lucy is in a candy factory. Immediately, workshop participants are able to describe the scene in great detail. If you know the episode, see if you can describe it. What was Lucy wearing? Who else was there? What were they doing? Lucy was with Ethel standing behind a conveyor belt attempting to place chocolates into boxes. To keep pace with the conveyor belt, they stuffed the candies into their mouths, uniforms and chef's hats.

When I ask my students to recall any three lines of dialog from the show, they are typically silent. We remember things that we *see* far better than things we *hear*. Effective visual aids can make your presentations more interesting while significantly increasing your listeners' retention of your material. This chapter will help you select, prepare, and use visual aids that are appropriate for your presentation.

Tips for Using Visual Aids

Tip #1. Use in a support role.
Many presentations turn into dull slide shows without much personality. Your visual aids should *support* and *clarify* your spoken message, not replace or duplicate it. Most often, your most powerful visual aid is *you!*

Tip #2. Keep 'em simple.
- Limit each visual to *one* main idea
- Bullet format with key words is better than complete sentences
- Minimize text, maximize graphics—charts, cartoons, diagrams, drawings, graphs and photos express more than words or numbers alone

"*A picture is worth a thousand words.*"

Tip #3. Make 'em BIG!
If people cannot easily see your visual aids, do not use them—they will only serve as visual *distractions*.

Tip #4. Talk to your audience, not to your visuals.
Direct your listeners' attention to your visual aids, but be sure to maintain eye contact with your audience.

Tip #5. Be prepared.
Pack your visual aids and handouts in "carry on" luggage if you're flying. Arrive early to learn equipment features and test everything. Be prepared to speak without your visual aids just in case! (Note: All bulbs eventually burn out!)

Examples of Bad and Good Visuals

AVOID THIS!

Audience Retention Rates
We remember very little of what we hear, perhaps as little as 10%. Visual aids can increase retention to about 50%. However, this visual aid has too much text and is not very visually appealing or memorable.

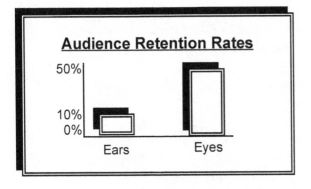

BETTER

BEST!

Overhead Transparencies

Advantages: Effective for small or large groups. Most lights can be left on.

Considerations: Some lights may need to be dimmed or turned off.

Tip #1. Apply the "7-by-7" rule: No more than seven words across and no more than seven lines of text.

Tip #2. Request or bring a spare bulb just in case.

Tip #3. Point to the *screen,* not to the machine. If you cannot reach the screen, you may wish to use a pointer.

Tip #4. Rather than turning off all the lights, if possible, dim or unscrew lights directly over the screen.

Tip #5. If possible, place the screen at a 45-degree angle and slightly to one side of the center of the room. This allows you to stand "center-stage" and more easily maintain listeners' attention while explaining the information being displayed.

Tip #6. Use at least 24-point fonts. If showing lots of detail, such as a flow chart, show the whole chart, then show an enlarged image of the portion you wish to discuss.

Tip #7. Frame transparencies for a professional look.

Tip #8. Arrive early and place a transparency on the projector to ensure it is focused, centered and straight. Mask-off with tape the glass area surrounding the frame to block unwanted light and provide a guide for placing each transparency.

PowerPoint® Presentations

Advantages: Software can help create professional, easily-modified shows.

Considerations: Apply Tips #1 - #6 from "Overhead Transparencies."

Tip #1. Don't overwhelm audiences with a dizzying, high-speed slide show. Aim for no more than one slide for every two minutes of presentation time.

Tip #2. Use a wireless lavaliere microphone so your hands are free to operate your computer and point. Use a *wireless* mouse so you can move freely.

Tip #3. Know how the software works and how to recover from computer glitches. Practice using all the features.

Tip #4. Incorporate other types of visual aids, such as a flip-chart to capture and illustrate ideas spontaneously or post pages on the walls for continuous reinforcement.

Tip #5. Press "B" to blank the screen and talk *without* a slide.

Tip #6. Don't duplicate your slides onto your handout. Consider fill-in-the blank handouts.

Tip #7. Have a backup plan in case Murphy's Law takes over!

Tip #8. Read "Death by PowerPoint!" by David Greenberg, available at www.davidgreenberg.com.

PowerPoint® is a trademark of Microsoft Corp.

35mm Slides

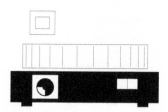

Advantages: Effective for small or large groups. You can use a rear-screen projector for a very polished look.

Considerations: Because the room must be quite dark, it is difficult to monitor audience reactions and build rapport. Difficult for listeners to take notes and remain alert in the dark. Your presentation is always in sequential order with no random access.

Tip #1. Apply Tips #1 - #6 from "Overhead Transparencies."

Tip #2. Number the slides on the frames in case you drop them.

Tip #3. You may want to have an assistant operate the projector and/or the room's lighting controls.

Tip #4. Practice extensively—including your remarks, the proper room lighting and projector features.

Tip #5. Be sure your slide carousel is compatible with the projector (you may wish to bring your own projector).

Flip Charts

3 T's:
Touch
Turn
Talk

Advantages: Easy to use. You can capture or illustrate ideas spontaneously. You can post pages on the walls for continuous reinforcement of ideas.

Considerations: Not effective for groups larger than 25-30 people. Writing can be slow—consider preparing some pages in advance or enlisting an assistant to help you capture ideas while you facilitate.

Tip #1. Apply the "3-T" Rule: *Touch* the flip chart, *Turn* toward the audience, *Talk* to the audience (do not talk to the chart).

Tip #2. Pause while writing to create suspense.

Tip #3. Test markers beforehand and dispose of dry markers.

Tip #4. Test the visibility of the colors you plan to use. Dark colors are most easily seen from a distance. Save red and light green for highlighting (i.e., circling, "X-ing out," etc.).

Tip #5. Write on every other page to prevent "ghosting," where people can see through to the next page.

Tip #6. Place sticky notes on the sides of prepared pages so you can find them quickly. Label them with the page's main idea.

Tip #7. Bring masking tape and push pins so you can post pages on the walls for continuous reinforcement of ideas.

Video Tapes and DVDs

Advantages: Can be very convincing and professionally prepared. Easy to transport.

Considerations: Preparation time, production expense, and availability of VCRs/DVD players and large monitors.

Tip #1. Cue the video to the starting position and test the volume as well as the visibility *before* participants arrive.

Tip #2. Plan your introductory and summary remarks. Tell viewers the length of the video and specific elements to watch for so they pay close attention.

Tip #3. Position monitor(s) for the entire group to see.

Tip #4. Dim lights slightly so participants can still take notes and remain alert.

Tip #5. Beware of showing videos directly after a meal—your audience might fall asleep.

Tip #6. Have a backup video in case the machine decides to eat the first one.

Handouts

Advantages: The audience focuses on you and your message rather than taking lots of notes. Useful for communicating details. Audiences perceive a higher value program when they receive a handout.

Considerations: Preparation time, timing of distribution, and the audience reading ahead rather than paying attention.

Handout Distribution Options

- At the beginning of your presentation:
Allows listeners to relax and not worry about taking notes. To prevent listeners from reading ahead, consider using a *fill-in-the-blank* format (see examples on the next page) or seal certain sections with peel-off labels and advise participants to remove the label only when you instruct them to do so.

- During your presentation:
Effective for revealing "surprise" information or having control over the flow of information. For large groups, ask for assistance to expedite distribution.

- At the end of your presentation:
Effective if you want listeners to listen more attentively rather than read ahead. Inform listeners of the material covered in your handout so they do not waste time taking unnecessary notes.

Sample Fill-in-the-Blank

The New Accounting System

1. Easier to Use
- _____
- ___% faster data entry
- _____

2. Better Reports
- ___ additional report options
- ___% faster printing
- _____

3. Saves Money
- _____
- ___% lower maintenance cost
- FREE _____

Our Financial Overview

Sales History:	Sales Projections:
1990:_____	2010: _____
1995:_____	2015: _____
2000:_____	2020: _____

To reach our goals, we must:
1. _____
2. _____
3. _____

Visual Aids Preparation Checklist

✓ To ensure my visual aids are effective, I have:

1. ___ developed visual aids that support (not duplicate) my spoken message

2. ___ kept them simple and easy to understand

3. ___ limited each visual aid to one main idea, when appropriate

4. ___ used bullet format with key words, when appropriate

5. ___ minimized text and maximized graphics

6. ___ made them large enough for everyone to easily see, even people in the back of the room

7. ___ practiced using them and the related equipment

8. ___ packed them in my "carry-on" luggage if I'm flying

9. ___ prepared and practiced a back-up plan in case Murphy's Law kicks in

Laughter is no enemy to learning.

Walt Disney

Chapter 9
Using Humor and Stories

Virtually any presentation can benefit from a bit of appropriate humor. The purpose of using humor in most presentations is not only to evoke laughter, but to illustrate a point or a lesson learned. The safest and most effective way to accomplish this is by sharing *anecdotes*—short, humorous stories often involving yourself.

People are persuaded more by emotion than reasoning, and stories are a powerful way to engage your audience's emotions. Take your abstract ideas and concepts and humanize them through stories. Use the basics of any good story—characters, setting, and a plot with a beginning, middle and an ending. The tips in this chapter are designed to help you incorporate stories that get a few laughs while driving home your more serious points.

Tips for Telling Stories

Tip #1. Use the "PIE" formula (example on next page)

P = State the *point* you wish to make

I = *Illustrate* the point with a story

E = *Emphasize* the importance to the audience (WII-FM?)

Tip #2. Skip the joke books—look at your life.

Your listeners want to know about *you*. Consider humorous incidents from your own life. Perhaps they were not funny when they occurred, but you can laugh at them now. If you can laugh at it, chances are your audience will, too.

Tip #3. Maintain a Humor/Story File.

It can be difficult to think of stories under the pressure of a presentation deadline, so start a "Humor/Story File" *today* and start noting your daily life experiences. Don't worry about what point an experience might make or if you'll ever share it. You never know when an item will fit perfectly into a future presentation.

Tip #4. If in doubt, leave it out.

Your story should never be at the expense of others. Period.

Tip #5. Practice your delivery.

Tell your story several times until you tell it the best way possible. Sneak stories into conversations and note how people react. Transition into your story with a phrase such as, "That reminds me of the time . . ." or "Let me share a story . . ."

Sample "PIE" Formula Story

Note: When I tell this story, the audience and I laugh, even though the experience was originally a painful one.

Point:
To achieve your dreams, you must not give-up.

Illustration:
When I was in the fifth grade, my dad enrolled me in Little League softball. This was a dream come true . . . for my dad! My first time at bat I swung three times and, to no one's amazement, I struck out. I felt humiliated. My second time at bat, I was so paralyzed with fear that I could not move. I stood there, motionless, as the first ball flew by. But instead of hearing "Strike one," I heard the umpire shout, "*Ball* one!" I had a plan! I remained motionless for the next few pitches and heard, "Ball two," "Ball three," and finally, "Ball four! Take your base." For the remaining games, I did not swing at the ball. Never! I figured my chances of getting to base were better this way. My teammates nicknamed me "Statue," and when I was at bat, they chanted, "Statue's up! Statue's up!"

Emphasize the importance to the audience:
I believe that too many people in this room are going through life like I went through Little League—not finding immediate success and giving-up. How many of you have given-up on a dream because you did not find immediate success? The kids who experienced Little League for *all* it had to offer were the ones who didn't quit—the ones who kept swinging. Sometimes they hit the ball, and sometimes they missed. Occasionally, one even hit a home run—something I never experienced, and something you will not experience if you don't keep swinging! Don't give-up on your dreams.

Exercise: Complete the following phrase in order to jog your memory and add some stories to your Humor/Story File. Jot down a few keywords from two or three of your life experiences and the lessons each story might illustrate.

> "When I think about my (mother/father/sister/
> brother/child/grandfather/grandmother/best
> friend/partner/schooldays/first job/most
> embarrassing moment/most difficult time/worst
> vacation/customer service experience), I can't help
> but recall the time . . ."

Story 1: _____

_____

Lesson(s): _____

_____

Story 2: _____

_____

Lesson(s): _____

_____

Story 3: _____

_____

Lesson(s): _____

_____

Using Humor and Stories Checklist

✓ To use humor and stories effectively, I will:

1. ___ use the "PIE" formula to incorporate stories

2. ___ skip the joke books and look at my own life

3. ___ maintain a Humor/Story File

4. ___ leave out any offensive stories

5. ___ practice my delivery

Words with a 'k' in them are funny.
If it doesn't have a 'k,' it's not funny.

Neil Simon

Don't be afraid to be outrageous;
the critics will shoot you down anyway.

Laurence Olivier

Chapter 10
Tricks to Eliminate Boring

Generally, people would rather be entertained than educated. You may not need to pull a rabbit out of your hat to maintain your audience's attention, but attention spans are short and you should know a few "tricks" to breathe life into your presentations and ensure your audience keeps listening.

One key to maintaining interest throughout a presentation is *variety*—variety in your voice, variety in your body language, variety in your visual aids, variety in your delivery methods. This chapter contains several tips and tricks to help you add some variety in order to maintain your listeners' attention and increase their retention. Also, be sure to read the next chapter, *Polishing Your Delivery*, for additional tips. Allow your creative juices to flow and have fun! Your listeners will appreciate it.

Tips for Eliminating Boring

Tip #1. Think "fun".

Review each point in your presentation and ask yourself, "How can I make this more fun? More interesting? More convincing? More memorable?" An executive I coached wanted his salespeople to think of the company more globally. He started his presentation with a world geography quiz. Anyone who volunteered an answer, right or wrong, received a chocolate globe. You can't go wrong when you give listeners chocolate!

Tip #2. Bring statistics to life.

Show listeners the magnitude of your statistics so they can clearly *see* the impact. Instead of just saying, "Our company sends 50 tons of paper to landfills every month," add "That's enough to fill the elevator banks in this office building from top to bottom every month!"

Tip #3. Use "Attention-Getters" throughout.

Review the Attention-Getters on page 33. They are not only effective ways to begin your presentation, but also to gain attention throughout as you introduce important ideas.

Tip #4. Do something unexpected.

Crush a soda can in your hands and say, "This is what the competition could do to us!" Ask everyone to stand on a chair and say, "Let's see things from a new perspective!" Be creative.

Tip #5. Play upbeat music.

Play upbeat music while people enter and exit the room. This helps energize the crowd and says, "This will be different."

Tip #6. Allow me to demonstrate . . .

People love to watch demonstrations. Instead of just talking about a process, *show* listeners how it's done.

Tip #7. Get 'em involved.

Ask *volunteers* to act-out a scenario. For example, you might say, "Joan, would you join me up front and act like an upset customer. Bob, would you demonstrate some methods to deal with her complaints." Lead the applause for their performances and ask the audience to comment on what they observed.

Tip #8. Start with an energizer.

For example, you could have everyone in the room shake hands with three people they have not yet met, or stand and share one of the best ideas they've learned so far with the people in the row behind them. Be creative!

Tip #9. Play games.

Especially in a lengthy program, a brief "game" can be a welcomed relief and a valuable learning experience. For example, play a game similar to *Family Feud* or *Jeopardy,* where team members compete for inexpensive prizes by answering questions about your topic.

Tip #10. Perform magic tricks.

Visit a magic shop and tell the salesperson the points in your presentation. He or she can help you learn a few easy tricks to capture attention and make your points more interesting.

Tip #11. Distribute toys.

Creativity increases when we bring out the "child" in people. Buy a few inexpensive toys (Play-Dough, Silly Putty, bubbles, etc.) and put them on participants' tables.

To be conscious that you are ignorant is a great step to knowledge.

Benjamin Disraeli

Chapter 11
Polishing Your Delivery

Nonverbal

Voice

Words

You have probably heard the phrase, "It's not what you say, but how you say it." Actually, both are extremely important and should be considered as you polish your presentation skills. The tips in this chapter are designed to help you polish your non-verbal skills or "body language," your speaking voice, and your word usage.

As you read this chapter, keep in mind that delivering a polished presentation is a skill, and like any other skill, it takes time to develop. Select one or two areas for improvement for each presentation, and over time, you will experience wonderful growth as a presenter.

Your Body Language

Tip #1. Dress for success.

Based on the way you are dressed, your listeners will make several decisions about you, right or wrong, concerning your level of education, income, success, trustworthiness and intelligence, to name just a few.

- Never dress more casually than your audience. The key is to look current, authoritative and appropriate for your audience and the occasion.

- Darker colors suggest power. Black is best saved for formal occasions.

- Contrasting and bright colors gain attention. Wear clothing that contrasts with the wall behind you so you stand out.

- Wear a minimum of jewelry, especially anything reflective, and especially if you tend to play with your jewelry.

Tip #2. If you're happy, tell your face!

As the saying goes, "It's written all over your face." Your face speaks volumes about your feelings toward your topic.
- Keep your face out of park! Show how you feel.
- A smile goes a long, long way. Practice if necessary.
- Remember: Your audience will mirror your expressions.

Tip #3. Stand proudly.

Your posture says a great deal about your level of confidence. Proper posture helps you breathe and project effectively, and serves as a foundation for effective gesturing and walking.

- Stand tall, as if to say, "I am confident. I am an authority. I am in control," not "I'm melting. . ., melting . . ., melting."

- Do not *lean* on the lectern for support.

- Plant your feet firmly until you feel you have gained appropriate attention and are ready to walk.

Tip #4. Gesture.

Use hand gestures to support your spoken words and express feelings—just like you do when you're talking with your friends. Note: The larger the audience, the larger the gestures.

If gesturing does not come easily to you while speaking, force at least one gesture into each sentence during your practice sessions. Soon, you will begin to gesture naturally before an audience.

Use your arms, hands and fingers to:
- Indicate which point you are discussing (1, 2 or 3)
- Indicate trends (up, down or flat)
- Describe sizes and shapes (small, large, or round)
- Point to charts and screens
- Emphasize your feelings (a clench fist suggests anger)
- Prompt (raise your hand when asking for a show of hands)

Tip #5. Make eye contact.

Strong eye contact bonds you to the audience and makes your presentation more personal as well as believable.

- Start and finish your presentation without referring to your notes.

- Hold "mini-conversations" with listeners (3 - 4 seconds). Rather than scanning the room with fleeting eye contact, finish an entire thought while looking at one person. Move to the next person when you finish the thought or sentence.

- When referring to your notes: Pause, glance at your notes, then look back up to speak—do not speak to your notes!

- Include people sitting in the back of the room. Let them know they are important and you want their attention.

- Monitor audience reactions and make any necessary changes. For example, if several people yawning, drop the statistics, vary your voice tone, cool the room or take a break.

Tip #6. Walk purposefully.

Walking *purposefully* during your talk builds rapport, hold listeners' attention, and burn-ups nervous energy.

- Deliver your opening and closing remarks "planted" center stage

- Move *forward* to connect with listeners and suggest an important point.

- Pause and move *sideways* as you transition from one main idea to another.

96

Put Some Fire in Your Voice!

Many presenters who are labeled "boring" could easily lose that title by developing a more dynamic speaking voice. Here are some tips to make the most of your speaking voice.

Tip #1. Speak conversationally.

Most people do not like to be *lectured* at. Speak to your audience as though you were discussing issues at your dinner table. For practice, read the newspaper to a friend in a heightened conversational tone as if you were reporting the news and experiment with your voice.

Tip #2. Pause, please.

Pause after making an important point (silently count "one- two"). This will help maintain your audience's attention and give them needed time to comprehend and "store" your idea before you present the next idea. The pause will seem longer to you than to your listeners.

Tip #3. *Stress* important words.

Identify and emphasize the *important* words in your message. For practice, read the sentence "I didn't say he cheated on his taxes," aloud five times, emphasizing a different word each time and note the changes in the meaning. If you tend to speak in a monotone or flat voice, incorporate more gestures into your talk. The broader and more emphatic your gestures, the more dynamic your voice will sound.

Tip #4. Vary your volume and rate.

Speed up and sloooow down to add interest. Speak loudly at times, and even whisper to get your audience on the edge of their chairs.

Tip #5. Don't speak too fast.

If you speak very fast, try increasing your eye contact. When you look into people's eyes, it's difficult to talk at a rate faster than they can easily understand.

Tip #6. Speak with E-N-T-H-U-S-I-A-S-M!

You cannot expect listeners to be enthusiastic about your ideas when you sound indifferent.

Tip #7. Warm-up your voice before you speak.

- Yawn. This loosens up your vocal cords.
- Wiggle your tongue. This loosens up your jaw and can help you from tripping over words.
- Take a deep breath and say, "ah . . ." for as long as you can. This helps soft-spoken speakers to project better.
- Avoid cold drinks, caffeine, and mints or foods with sugar before you speak (these can adversely impact your voice).
- Keep a glass and pitcher of room-temperature water nearby while you speak. Sip the water during some of your pauses—not only will this help your voice, it can add dramatic impact.

Choose Your Words Carefully

Although it is best not to plan most presentations word-for-word, there are times when a well-chosen word or phrase can add significant impact to your presentation. The following guidelines are provided with the assistance of respected Professor of Communication, Dr. John Gentile.

Tip #1. Use a basic vocabulary.

Apply the "KISS" principle—*Keep It Simply Stated!* Avoid using a big word when a little one will do nicely. If there is a chance someone in your audience is unfamiliar with certain terms or acronyms, explain or define them.

Tip #2. Use the pronouns "you" and "your."

The pronouns *you* and *your* are "ear-perkers." Instead of saying, "Here are the benefits . . .," say, "Here is how *you* benefit," or ask, "How will *your* company benefit?" Occasionally, use the names of audience members, such as: "Let's assume that *Mary* (an audience member) wants a new car . . ."

Tip #3. Paint vivid pictures.

Choose words that help your audience visualize your ideas as *images*. Find words that have strong sensory appeal—think not only in terms of the sense of sight, but taste, smell, touch and hot or cold. Instead of just saying, "This year's conference will be held at the beach," add, "Picture the warm ocean breeze massaging your face as the cool, wet sand oozes between your toes and the blood-red sunset dips behind the mountain top."

Tip #4. Develop clear transitions.

Audiences need your help in moving with you from idea to idea. Bring them along with you by saying something along the lines of "Now that we understand the importance of [first main point], let's turn to our attention to [next main point]," or "Now that I've discussed [first main point], I want to consider [next main point]," or "Once we've mastered [first main point], the next challenge is [next main point]."

Tip #5. Preface important ideas.

Grab listeners' attention by prefacing key ideas with phrases like:
- "Here is the secret weapon of top achievers in our field . . ."
- "If you remember only one thing today, remember this . . ."
- "Here's the bottom line . . ."
- "Two people in the world know what I'm about to tell you."
- "This next slide will shock many of you."
- "You will want to write down this next idea."

Tip #6. Develop simple acronyms.

Simple acronyms can help listeners remember your ideas. Review the many acronyms used throughout this book (Chapters 12 - 15) and develop some of your own. Keep them as simple as possible.

Tip #7. Sprinkle quotations.

Quotations can add credibility and interest to your presentation. Quote a well-known expert in your field, a respected person from history, or for uniqueness, even your favorite relative or teacher. If the person is unfamiliar to the group, provide any necessary background information.

Tip #8. Ask questions.

Review important statements in your presentation to see if you can incorporate a question to gain attention. For example, rather than just stating, "This is important because . . .," first ask rhetorically, "Why is this so important?" Pause slightly, then tell listeners the answer. If you desire a response to your question, pause longer and, if appropriate, raise your hand to encourage participation.

Tip #9. Use Analogies, Metaphors, and Similes.

These devices help listeners understand an idea through a comparison. It is particularly useful for speakers wishing to assist an audience in understanding an unfamiliar idea by comparing it to a familiar one.

Advertisers who must convey ideas quickly are masters at using these devices. A few years ago, a car manufacturer used the following analogy to convey the benefits of their new car design: The spokesperson asked viewers, "If you want to make a chair as stable as possible, where would you position the legs?" He answered, "At the corners, of course." He then asked, "If you want to make a car as stable as possible, where would you position the wheels?" Once again, he answered, "At the corners." He continued, "That's what we have done on our new cars with 'cab-forward' design." Viewers could now grasp the newly introduced concept of car stability.

Similes and metaphors are figures of speech comparing two unlike things. "My love is *like* a red, red rose," is a simile. "My love *is* a red, red rose" is a metaphor. Examples of similes from the world of advertising include "Like a good neighbor, State Farm is there," and "Like a rock" (Chevy trucks). Examples of metaphors include a car ad from Audi, "Think of it as a convertible rocket," and an ad for a Sears Kenmore freezer that reads: "It isn't a freezer. It's a glacial grand ballroom where french vanilla ice cream and long, luscious crab legs have 20% more room to waltz." For practice, think of how your idea is similar to a marriage, planting a garden, raising children, making a pizza, exercising, going on a diet, etc.

Tip #10. Use classical rhetoric techniques.

While the Latin names for these language devices may sound strange, the ideas behind them are familiar—and they work. With some thought you can create memorable phrases that sum up your main theme and that your audiences will carry home with them. The following devices should be used with moderation:

- **Anaphora:** Beginning phrases or sentences with the same or very similar words. For example, Franklin D. Roosevelt's *War Message* of Dec. 8, 1941:

> Last night Japanese forces attacked Hong Kong.
> Last night Japanese forces attacked Guam.
> Last night Japanese forces attacked the Philippine Islands.
> Last night Japanese forces attacked Wake Island.

- **Chiasmus:** This is the inversion of sentence order. It emphasizes an idea by stating a clause and then inverting its established order and, thereby, changing it's meaning. For example, John F. Kennedy's inaugural address telling Americans "Ask not what your country can do for you, ask what you can do for your country."

Polishing Your Delivery Checklist

✓ To be effective with my body language, I will:

1. ___ dress for success
2. ___ use appropriate facial expressions, including smiling
3. ___ stand proudly
4. ___ incorporate natural gestures
5. ___ make strong eye contact
6. ___ walk purposefully (and also stay planted at times)

✓ To be effective with my voice, I will:

1. ___ speak conversationally
2. ___ pause to allow listeners to digest my ideas
3. ___ stress important words
4. ___ vary my volume and rate
5. ___ speak at a rate listeners can easily understand
6. ___ speak with enthusiasm
7. ___ warm-up my voice before I speak

✓ To be effective with my words, I will:

1. ___ use a basic vocabulary
2. ___ use the pronouns "you" and "your"
3. ___ paint vivid pictures
4. ___ develop clear transitions
5. ___ preface important ideas
6. ___ develop simple acronyms
7. ___ sprinkle interesting quotations
8. ___ ask questions to gain attention
9. ___ use analogies, metaphors, and similes
10. ___ use classical rhetoric techniques

Be sincere, be brief, be seated.

Franklin Delano Roosevelt

Section III
Quick Formulas
for
Short Presentations

Heeere's Johnny!

Ed McMahon's introduction of Johnny Carson
for 30 years on *The Tonight Show*

Chapter 12
Introducing a Guest Speaker

The speaker introduction is an often overlooked, but vitally important part of setting the stage for a successful presentation. When you accept an invitation to speak, it is usually in your best interest to provide the person introducing you with your own introduction (large font and double-spaced). Send your introduction a few days before the presentation to give your introducer time to practice. Most introducers will be glad you volunteered to take care of this important detail.

If you are introducing the guest speaker, ask the speaker for an introduction or prepare one using the formula in this chapter. Whether you're the speaker or the introducer, this chapter will help you set the right tone for the presentation.

The "SIN" Formula

It is a "sin" to poorly introduce a speaker, so use the "SIN" formula to ensure your introductions are effective. As long as all the components are covered, the order is up to you.

S = Subject
State the subject or title of the presentation.

I = Importance
State why the subject is important to the audience, and state why the speaker is important (the speaker's credentials).

N = Name
State the speaker's name (spell it phonetically in your notes).

Tips for Introducing a Speaker

Tip #1. Practice.
Read the introduction *out loud* a few times before show time.

Tip #2. Lead the applause and greet the speaker.
Audiences are sometimes reluctant to applaud, so get it started. Greet the speaker with a handshake, then sit within eye contact of the speaker for possible cues.

Tip #3. Be ready when the speaker is finished.
Stand, lead the applause, return to the front of the room, shake the speaker's hand, and thank him or her for the presentation.

Sample "SIN" Introduction

Subject:
"Our next presenter will tell us about an exciting new tool that can make each of our jobs easier! This afternoon, we will explore the advantages of replacing our old accounting software system."

Importance:
"This presentation will be important to each of you because each of you uses the accounting system, to either enter data or generate reports. We know you'll want to be part of the decision-making process."

"Our presenter is highly qualified to recommend a new system. He is a Certified Public Accountant. He has been with our company for ten years, and has worked with our current accounting system for five of those years. He knows first-hand how we operate, and he has spent the last three months reviewing our needs and speaking with several accounting software manufacturers."

Name:
"Help me welcome Division Manager Stan Czachowski."
(Spelled phonetically in notes "Cha-how-ski")

Speaker Introduction Worksheet

Write your speaker introduction below.

Subject:

_____

_____

_____

Importance:

(Importance of Subject):

_____

_____

_____

(Importance of Speaker):

_____

_____

_____

Name: _____

Phonetic spelling (if necessary): _____

Speaker Introduction Checklist

✓ In my speaker introduction, I will include the:

1. ___ subject and/or title of the presentation

2. ___ importance of the presentation to the audience

3. ___ importance of the speaker (credentials)

4. ___ name of the speaker (spelled phonetically)

✓ When introducing a speaker, I will:

1. ___ practice the introduction out loud

2. ___ lead the applause, greet the speaker, and be ready possible for cues

3. ___ be ready to stand when the speaker is finished, lead the applause, shake the speaker's hand, and thank him or her for the presentation

*You can't sweep people off their feet
if you can't be swept off your own.*

Clarence Day

Chapter 13
Persuasive and Motivational Presentations

When preparing this type of presentation, remember that listeners are seeking to satisfy *their* needs—not yours. You must have a solid understanding of your audience so you can phrase your appeal in terms of what will motivate them. It is also important to realize that logic alone is often *not* enough to motivate people to take action.

If appealing to logic was enough, then laundry detergent ads would simply show that their detergent cleans the clothes better than other brands. Instead, these ads also show us how proud we will *feel* when our child wears a bright white softball uniform, or how embarrassed we will *feel* by a "ring around the collar." Look at what automobile ads really sell—*excitement, power, prestige.* Advertisers know how to appeal to our logic *and* our emotions. If you hope to persuade listeners to accept your ideas and take action, you must do the same.

The "ANSVA" Persuasive Formula

A = Attention
Gain your listeners' *attention* with a compelling story or other appropriate attention-getter and make them want to listen to what follows (see page 33, "Attention-Getters").

N = Need
Demonstrate the *need* for what you are about to propose. Paint a picture of the need or the problem as it exists today (analyze your audience beforehand to ensure that they will appreciate this need and feel motivated to do something about it). Include facts, examples, and stories which highlight the need for a change and appeal to listeners both *logically* and *emotionally*.

S = Satisfaction/Solution
Offer a solution which clearly *satisfies* the need or problem you have described. Support your solution with facts.

V = Visualization
Use vivid descriptions and strong imagery to help listeners *visualize* a picture in their minds of what could happen if they implement your solution. You may also want to paint a contrasting picture of what could happen if they do not implement your solution.

A = Action
Call for *action*. What do you want listeners to do? Be specific. Provide an easy manner to take action (provide a phone number, sales agreement, form letter, petition, etc.). The easier it is for listeners to act, the greater the odds that they will act.

Sample "ANSVA" Presentation

Attention:
"What would you do with an extra hour or two every month?"

Need:
"You are wasting at least an hour or two every month using our outdated accounting software. Reports take as much as 30 minutes to generate and are often difficult to understand, making your job stressful and making you look bad. It takes nearly two weeks to train a data entry clerk, the system goes down at least once each week, and its annual maintenance costs could pay for a nice vacation for each of us."

Satisfaction/Solution:
"The solution is to replace the system with one which can better meet our needs while still staying within our budget."

Visualization:
"Imagine being able to request and receive easy-to-understand reports in just minutes. Imagine feeling at ease, rather than stressed-out waiting in front of a printer. Imagine a new employee being able to enter data with a minimum amount of training, freeing you to do other things. Imagine feeling confident that the information you use to make financial decisions is accurate. Imagine what you could do with an extra hour or two every month."

Action:
"Please allow me three weeks to research new systems and report my findings to you at the next staff meeting."

Persuasive Presentation Worksheet

 Jot down some key words and phrases for your persuasive presentation using the "ANSVA" formula.

Attention:

_____

_____

Need:

_____

_____

Satisfaction/Solution:

_____

_____

Visualization:

_____

_____

Action:

_____

_____

Chapter 14
Presenting a Status Report:
You're the S-T-A-R-R!

As a manager, supervisor or employee, you may be asked to present status or progress reports. These types of reports may be given, for example, at staff meetings or perhaps at conferences with upper management. This can be your chance to let your "STARR" shine! For these situations, use the "STARR" formula in this chapter to deliver a well-organized and informative presentation.

The "STARR" Formula

S = Situation

Paint a vivid picture of the situation you experienced.

T = Task

Tell listeners what your specific task was in this situation.

A = Action Steps

State the specific action steps you took. In other words, how did you complete the task?

R = Results

Paint a vivid picture of the results you achieved. Show your enthusiasm for the positive results or your disappointment with the negative results.

R = Recommendations

What should listeners do now? Be specific.

Here's how I did it

Sample "STARR" Presentation

Situation:

"Here's the *situation:* Our data entry clerks were complaining that the accounting software was very slow to learn and use. It crashed an average of once each week. Upper management was complaining that the reports took too long to produce, were difficult to understand and sometimes unreliable."

Task:

"My *task* was to find a new system which would better meet our needs and still meet our budget constraints."

Action Steps:

"Here are the *action* steps I took:
- First, I interviewed all the data-entry clerks to discover their likes and dislikes about the old system.
- Second, I interviewed management to discover their likes and dislikes about the old system.
- Third, I listed all the features we wanted and mailed 'Request for Bids' to the top ten accounting software manufacturers.
- Finally, I reviewed each of their bids and compared them to the features we needed and our budget constraints."

Results:

"The *result* is that ABC Software Systems, one of the highest-regarded software manufacturers, can give us everything we want and stay within our budget!"

Recommendations:

"I *recommend* that we allow ABC Software Systems to begin designing our new system next week."

119

Status Report Worksheet

 Jot down some key words and phrases for your status report using the "STARR" formula.

Situation:

_____

_____

Task:

_____

_____

Action Steps:

_____

_____

Results:

_____

_____

Recommendations:

_____

_____

Chapter 15
Accepting an Award

When you receive an award, a promotion or anything where you want to say more than a mere "thank you," use the "TCUT" formula and you will be ready to deliver a brief acceptance speech with style.

The "TCUT" Formula

T = Thank you
Thank the people who are recognizing you.

C = Credit
Recognize others who should receive credit.

U = Use
Tell how you will use the award or gift.

T = Thank you again
Add an extra "thank you" at the end.

Sample "TCUT" Presentation

Thank you: *"Thank you* Mike for this award."

Credit: "The *credit* really goes to the entire project team—Charlie, Jay, Sue, and Carol."

Use: "I am going to *use* this award to remind me of the challenges we overcame . . ."

Thank you again: "Thank you, again."

Acceptance Speech Worksheet

 Jot down some key words and phrases for your acceptance speech using the "TCUT" formula.

Thank you:

_____

_____

Credit:

_____

_____

_____

_____

Use:

_____

_____

_____

"Thank you, again."

123

Every vital organization owes its birth and life to an exciting and daring idea.

James B. Conant

Section IV
101 Secrets of
Top Professional Speakers

The National Speakers Association

The National Speakers Association is an association of approximately four thousand professional speakers dedicated to advancing the art and value of experts who speak professionally. As a member of NSA for many years, I have had the good fortune of meeting, listening to, and learning from some of the world's top professional speakers.

When I asked these respected speakers to contribute to this book, I was overwhelmed by their willingness to share. I believe their giving attitude contributes greatly to their success, and I thank them for their tremendous help.

Several of the contributing speakers have earned the designation of "Certified Speaking Professional." CSP is the highest earned designation presented by NSA. Currently, only 7 percent of NSA members hold this designation. I earned the title in 1998. Some of the contributing speakers have earned the designation of "Council of Peers Award for Excellence." The CPAE is an award for platform excellence, and is awarded to a maximum of five people each year. Regardless of their titles, each of the speakers included in this chapter is dedicated to mastering his or her craft and works diligently to ensure the success of every presentation.

No matter what type of speaking you do, you will find several tips in this chapter to help increase your effectiveness. If you would like to observe some of the best speakers in the business, if you have aspirations of becoming a professional speaker, or if your organization ever needs a professional speaker, contact NSA headquarters at 602-968-2552.

Top Professional Speakers'
Secrets for
Reducing Speech Anxiety

Tip #1. Your nervous energy about speaking in public is not a poison to be eliminated or ignored. It is a power to be unleashed. Pay the preparation-price, and celebrate the butterflies!

- Stephen M. Gower, CSP
Author of *Celebrate the Butterflies —
Presenting with Confidence in Public*

Tip #2. Trust your knowledge, skill, and preparation. Then have fun!

- Austin McGonigle, CSP

Tip #3. Stop caring so much! Rise above the approval of others. Say what you say because you love to say it and have fun saying it. The only worthwhile evaluation comes from knowing in your gut that you served your audience well by giving them your best.

- Larry Winget, CSP, CPAE
Author of *The Simple Way to Success*

Tip #4. Always call back a success in your mind before you speak. It will give you added confidence.

- Scott Friedman, CSP
Past President, Colorado Speakers Association
Author of *Using Humor for a Change*

Tip #5. Laminate 10 of your best testimonials in 18 point type. On the morning of a challenging program, read them as you get dressed and ready to go.

- Barbara L. Pagano, Ed.S.
Past President, National Speakers Assn., Georgia Chapter

Tip #6. Be yourself. No other speaker can do a speech like you.

- Patti A. Wood, CSP

Tip #7. I joined Toastmasters to learn how to deal with my nerves. John Weeks, a gentleman who belonged to Toastmasters since the invention of sound, took me aside and offered two gold nuggets of advice: "Don't call it nerves. Call it excitement!" and "The audience wants to see you succeed. Learn to trust them."

- Doug Smart, CSP
Author of *TimeSmart*

Tip #8. In a crisis, slow down or just hold still until you can think clearly again.

- Stephen G. Preas, MD

Tip #9. Go into the restroom, look in the mirror and say, "I am the best possible speaker that could have been asked to speak on this particular day for this particular group."

- Austin McGonigle, CSP

Tip #10. If you are preoccupied with whether or not the audience will like you, the odds are they won't. If you are preoccupied with how your message can make their lives better, they'll love you.

- Doug Smart, CSP
Author of *TimeSmart*

Tip #11. Though it may be tempting to confess your anxiety to your audience, don't do it! Your audience wants to see someone who appears confident and speaks with conviction. The speakers who rise to the top are those who use their confidence to make their audience comfortable and attentive, in a powerful state of learning.

- Dan Thurmon, CSP

Tip #12. Remember: The only perfect speakers are in training films.

- Terry Paulson, Ph.D., CSP, CPAE
Author of *They Shoot Managers Don't They?*

Top Professional Speakers'
Secrets for
Speech Preparation

Tip #13. The primary reason why speakers fail is lack of preparation. Practice may not make perfect, but it does make one better. Enough practice makes one great. Speaking, like any other worthwhile endeavor, requires much practice and preparation.

- Mark Sanborn, CSP, CPAE
Author of *TeamBuilt: Making Teamwork Work*

Tip #14. Remember: Tell 'em what you're going to tell 'em; Tell 'em; Tell 'em what you've told 'em.

- Eleanor M. Fountain, Ph.D.
Author of *Success Through Assertiveness*

Tip #15. Don't memorize! Just organize! A memorized speech sounds canned. Organize your notes and know your material.

- Shep Hyken, CSP
Coauthor of the *Only the Best* series

Tip #16. Read good novels—especially those told in the first person—as a way of seeing how good writers tell first-person narratives. This "voice" will help you shape the words you use and make them more lively.

- Lou Heckler, CSP, CPAE

Tip #17. Always write your own introduction.

- Anthony B. Thomas
"The Spark Plug"

Tip #18. Tailor your introduction to the audience in order to establish credibility and acceptance.

- Eleanor M. Fountain, Ph.D.
Author of *Success Through Assertiveness*

Tip #19. Engage your ears before you employ your mouth. Always do your homework before every presentation.

- Jim Meisenheimer, CSP
Author of *Forty-Seven Ways to Sell Smarter*

Tip #20. Know how your audience will be dressed, and dress similarly. The symbolism of dressing similarly shows you understand and fit in with their culture.

- Jim Cairo
Author of *The Power of Effective Listening*

Tip #21. Arrive at the meeting room early enough to get all your preparation finished well before audience members arrive. Make the meeting room "your own" so you can feel comfortable in it, increase your confidence, and welcome your "guests" in a relaxed manner as they arrive.

- Ken Futch, CSP
Past President, National Speakers Assn., Georgia Chapter

Tip #22. During the development of stories, constantly ask yourself, "So what?" As in, so what does the audience care about this?

- Shirley Garrett, Ph.D.
Past President, National Speakers Assn., Georgia Chapter

Tip #23. Write your speech from the inside out. Don't get stuck trying to come up with a clever opening. Write the body first and the opening and closing will come to you.

- Eric Chester, CSP
Author of the *Teen Power* series

Tip #24. Under-promise and over-deliver to *all* groups, not just the larger ones.

- D. J. Harrington
Author of *Giggle's Christmas Lesson*

Tip #25. Turn strangers into friends. Call a few audience members well in advance of your program and introduce yourself. Refer to them by name during your presentation. Also, mingle and greet the audience as they enter the room.

- Jane Riley
Past President, National Speakers Assn., Georgia Chapter
Author of *Quiggles! Quips, Quotes and Giggles*

Tip #26. For out-of-town engagements, never take the last flight out! If it's delayed or canceled, this can significantly increase your stress. You want to arrive calm and able to focus on your audience and your message.

- Jim Cairo
Author of *The Power of Effective Listening*

Tip #27. Write your speech in an outline and bullet-point format—not word-for-word. Otherwise, if you forget a word, it's tough to recover.

- Lisa Ford, CPAE
Author of *How to Give Exceptional Customer Service*

Tip #28. Get a mentor, be a mentor; you learn faster when you are a student and teacher at the same time.

- Stephen G. Preas, MD

What you are speaks so loudly,
I cannot hear what you are saying.

Ralph Waldo Emerson

Top Professional Speakers' Secrets for
The Speech Environment

Tip #29. The hotel concierge is your best friend. He or she can find anything you need. Please remember to tip them.

- Dale Irvin, CSP, CPAE
Author of *Laughter Doesn't Hurt*

Tip #30. When speaking in a hotel, place duct tape over the door latches so they don't make distracting noises if people enter or exit the room.

- Stephen M. Gower, CSP
Author of *Celebrate the Butterflies —*
Presenting with Confidence in Public

Tip #31. Always take responsibility for a new battery in your wireless microphone. Even when they say, "only used once," that is too much. Carry extras and make that a habit.

- Rosita Perez, CPAE
Author of *The Music Is You: A Guide to*
Thinking Less and Feeling More

Tip #32. Don't be a pain in the meeting planner's neck! If you are, he or she will remember that. If you are not, he or she will remember that, too.

- Connie Podesta, CSP
Coauthor of *How to Be the Person*
Successful Companies Fight to Keep

Tip #33. Never speak following a long cocktail hour.

- Nido Qubein, CSP, CPAE
Past President, National Speakers Association
Author of *How to Be a Great Communicator*

Tip #34. For workshops, arrange your seating "team style," with groups of tables that hold approximately five or six people each. This allows for better interaction amongst participants than "U-shape" configurations.

- Mike Stewart, CSP
President, National Speakers Assn., Georgia Chapter

Tip #35. Pay attention to the "elephant in the corner." If you are hot, the audience probably is, too. Ask them. Then appoint someone to take care of adjusting the temperature *before* people begin to fan themselves and fall asleep.

- Rosita Perez, CPAE

Tip #36. Bring a roll of masking tape to block off the last rows of chairs to force people to sit toward the front. A scattered audience brings scattered results.

- Mark Mayberry
Author of *In the Company of Entrepreneurs*

Tip #37. Set the room with one less row than you think you will need. It forces people to move forward. When it fills, put in the last row. This makes it look like you had "standing room only."

> - Jeff Slutsky, CSP
> Author of *Street Fighter Marketing*

Tip #38. For specific or unusual room arrangements, send detailed floor plans based on the specific room. Make sure to contact the supervisor of room setup, not just the meeting manager or sales department.

> - Robert Alan Black, Ph.D., CSP
> Author of *Broken Crayons: Break Your Crayons and Draw Outside the Lines*

Tip #39. Show up for your presentation early and remember to check the "S.A.L.T." Check the *seating* configuration, the *audio visual* equipment, the *lighting,* and the *temperature* (note: the temperature will rise as the crowd enters the room).

> - Ed Metcalf, Ph.D.

Tip #40. Learn the names of the audiovisuals and technical staff at the meeting site. They are your shield against the "techno-gremlins."

> - Susan Harvey

Tip #41. Be flexible. The meeting planner is overwhelmed with responsibilities, and by being flexible you will make their job easier. They will remember that!

- W. Mitchell, CSP, CPAE
Author of *It Isn't What Happens to You,*
It's What You Do About It

Tip #42. If speaking in a hotel, find out what groups will be on either side of your partition walls. If you're going to have a marching band next door to fire up the troop, you had better be prepared. Have a couple of ad-libs ready.

- Jeff Slutsky, CSP
Author of *Street Fighter Marketing*

Tip #43. Before a break, give a positive "spin" on what will be covered after the break. Build expectations so participants are compelled to return.

- Naomi Rhode, CSP, CPAE
Past President, National Speakers Association

Tip #44. Eliminate the "moat effect." Be sure the first row of seats is close to the stage area so you can connect better with listeners.

- Mark Mayberry
Author of *In the Company of Entrepreneurs*

Tip #45. If you need to gain the attention of a noisy crowd, rather than saying something like, "Your attention please!" or "Shh," softly blow into the microphone. This noise is unlike the noise generated by the competing conversations, and conversations will come to an abrupt halt. Another technique for gaining the attention of a noisy crowd is to announce: "If you can hear me, please clap twice." Repeat this a few times, and gradually your entire audience will be applauding and you're ready to begin.

- Ken Futch, CSP
Past President, National Speakers Assn., Georgia Chapter

Tip #46. If speaking at a luncheon or dinner, ask the person in charge of catering to stop all serving and clearing dishes just before you are introduced. Otherwise, this can be very distracting.

- Jane Riley
Past President, National Speakers Assn., Georgia Chapter
Author of *Quiggles! Quips, Quotes and Giggles*

Top Professional Speakers' Secrets for Speech Content

Tip #47. At the start of every speech, your primary challenge is to break preoccupation. Each audience member is preoccupied with their own thoughts and concerns. A powerful, attention-grabbing beginning is critical.

- Mark Sanborn, CSP, CPAE
Author of *TeamBuilt: Making Teamwork Work*

Tip #48. Develop ways to be more entertaining as a speaker. That does not mean just telling jokes—although that works well also. Use humor, stories, visual aids, music, handouts and more. Your concern is the audience's boredom level. Your "competition" comes from MTV and major motion pictures. Do we stand a chance when our audience just saw Terminator 3 with $50 billion in special effects? Yes, if we work to go beyond being a talking head behind a lectern!

- Shep Hyken, CSP
Coauthor of the *Only the Best* series

Tip #49. Use stories from your own life. Stories penetrate and are retained. Your own stories are easy to remember and will be new to the audience.

- Terry Paulson, Ph.D., CSP, CPAE
Author of *They Shoot Managers Don't They?*

Tip #50. People don't remember your points; they remember your illustrations. If they can remember your story, then they will be able to remember the point or lesson that the story teaches. Stories are like mental coat-pegs: a place for listeners to hang ideas.

- Mark Sanborn, CSP, CPAE
Author of *TeamBuilt: Making Teamwork Work*

Tip #51. A good speaker looks for ways to involve the audience. A good story provides an avenue. As I tell a story, I often ask questions that keep the audience responding. I'll reach a point in the story and ask something like, "What do you think he did next?" If the audience is really with me, the answer will immediately pop into their minds, and I can tell, just by watching them, that I've connected.

- Nido Qubein, CSP, CPAE
Past President, National Speakers Association
Author of *How to Be a Great Communicator*

Tip #52. Discover your uniqueness. Each of us has a unique angle or outlook. We all have unique stories to tell. Stop trying to fit the mold so you end up sounding like everyone else. Do your own stuff—be yourself.

- Larry Winget, CSP, CPAE
Author of *The Simple Way to Success*

Tip #53. Remember: facts tell; stories sell. Tell stories to anchor your points.

- Willie Jolley, CSP
Author of *It Only Takes a Minute to Change Your Life!*

Tip #54. Actively seek and plan personal growth experiences that will increase your opportunities for story material and enhance your sense of well-being. Personal energy builds when you are consistently working on your own goals and dreams.

- Glenna Salsbury, CSP, CPAE
Author of *The Art of the Fresh Start*

Tip #55. Make a special effort to contact the competitors of the company you are addressing. Nothing gets attention like mentioning their arch-rivals.

- Harvey Mackay, CPAE
Author of NY Times Bestseller
Dig Your Well Before You're Thirsty

Tip #56. Make sure your statistics are accurate.

- Shirley Garrett, Ph.D.
Past President, National Speakers Assn., Georgia Chapter

Tip #57. If you provide a handout, include your name, company name, phone number, fax number, Website, E-mail address and 800 number. You want it to be easy for audience members to contact you.

- Ed Metcalf, Ph.D.

Tip #58. Tie a prop into your talks. I teach a class called "No Stone Unturned" and give every participant a small polished stone to carry for the next 90 days as a reminder of the talk and the goals that we set in the class.

- D. J. Harrington
Author of *Giggle's Christmas Lesson*

Tip #59. Only say what you love to say. Dump all the material that you aren't absolutely passionate about. People are only interested in your passion.

- Larry Winget, CSP, CPAE
Author of *The Simple Way to Success*

Tip #60. Speak with passion and power! Talk about what you know about and what you are passionate and exited about, not what is today's newest fad or hot topic.

- Willie Jolley, CSP
Author of *It Only Takes a Minute to Change Your Life!*

Tip #61. Create your own "signature" audience involvement exercises which people will recognize as uniquely yours.

- Robert Alan Black, Ph.D., CSP
Author of *Broken Crayons: Break Your Crayons
and Draw Outside the Lines*

Tip #62. Always use something in your presentation that you do not include in the handout—a poem, a list of books and authors, reference articles—that you will offer to send participants if they give you a business card. This helps you build a database of people who have heard you speak.

- Ed Metcalf, Ph.D.

Tip #63. Collect material that moves you! Your audience listens to your voice, but your connection needs to occur mentally, emotionally, physically and spiritually.

- Glenna Salsbury, CSP, CPAE
Author of *The Art of the Fresh Start*

Tip #64. Start strong and end strong. People remember your open and close, so make them good.

- Willie Jolley, CSP
Author of *It Only Takes a Minute to Change Your Life!*

Tip #65. Use the "PIE" concept for greater impact. State your *Point*. *Illustrate* your point with a personal story, analogy, etc. *Emphasize* the connection between the illustration and the point for greater clarity and understanding.

- Dick Biggs
Past President, National Speakers Assn., Georgia Chapter
Author of *If Life is a Balancing Act,*
Why Am I So Darn Clumsy?

Tip #66. If your time is shortened, edit, don't speed up.

- Shirley Garrett, Ph.D.
Past President, National Speakers Assn., Georgia Chapter

Tip #67. Turn off your wireless microphone before going to the bathroom.

- Dale Irvin, CSP, CPAE
Author of *Laughter Doesn't Hurt*

Tip #68. You didn't do it alone. Acknowledge those who have helped you—the meeting planner, those whom you may have interviewed, the person who picked you up at the airport. It helps to personalize the moment and shows your appreciation.

- Rosita Perez, CPAE
Author of *The Music is You: A Guide to*
Thinking Less and Feeling More

*Say what you think,
but feel what you say.*

William Jennings Bryant

Top Professional Speakers' Secrets for
Speech Delivery

Tip #69. Say it like you know it!

> \- Anthony B. Thomas
> "The Spark Plug"

Tip #70. Don't tell the story . . . BE the story! When using a personal story as an illustration, act out the parts to make the moment come alive.

> \- Lou Heckler, CSP, CPAE

Tip #71. The best advice on speaking I ever got was more than 20 years ago from David Johnson, then an Ohio legislator. He told me that every audience wants to be entertained. I have found that education is usually best delivered on the wings of entertainment.

> \- Mark Sanborn, CSP, CPAE
> Author of *TeamBuilt: Making Teamwork Work*

Tip #72. A speaker's obligation is to inspire, not motivate. Inspire means "to stimulate thinking." Motivate means "to cause action." The audience will be more self-motivated to act on your message based on the passion and sincerity of your inspiration.

> \- Dick Biggs
> Past President, National Speakers Assn., Georgia Chapter

Tip #73. For improved rhythm, take the time to watch how successful speakers draw in their audiences by periods of silence and by building to a crescendo as the talk progresses.

- David Ryback, Ph.D.
Author of *Putting Emotional Intelligence to Work*

Tip #74. Don't adopt a "stage persona." People watch you before and after you are on stage, and they want to see the same person. They want you to live your message. For example, if you talk about commitment, you had better keep yours.

- Connie Podesta, CSP
Author of *How to Be the Person Successful Companies Fight to Keep*

Tip #75. Keep your throat relaxed by drinking warm, rather than hot or cold drinks, prior to speaking. I suggest "Throat Coat" tea, available at most health food stores.

- Myra McElhaney

Tip #76. Be alive and be yourself. They're not paying you to be someone else.

- Jim Meisenheimer, CSP
Author of *Forty-Seven Ways to Sell Smarter*

Tip #77. I use every conceivable prop in the business including clown suits, magic, kazoos, harmonicas, bumper stickers, train horns, masks, hats, a stuffed monkey, whips, sirens, poker cards, rubber grips, you name it. My basic philosophy is "All I want out of life is an unfair advantage."

- Michael Aun, CSP
Author of *The Toastmasters International Guide to Successful Speaking*

Tip #78. As part of my preparation for producing a one-man play on Abraham Lincoln, I took a number of acting classes and studied the concepts and techniques that great actors use. One of the most powerful of these is what they call "being in the moment" or "being in the now." When you are in the moment, or in the now, you do not allow your thoughts to wander even for an instant to the future or the past—to what you might be doing tomorrow or what you might have done two days ago. Your thoughts are smack dab in that moment. This is a very difficult concept to put into practice, but if you can sustain it even for a short while, it is a very, very powerful technique for one-on-one communications and on the platform.

- Gene Griessman, Ph.D.
Author of *Time Tactics of Very Successful People*

Tip #79. End your question-and-answer session time before the questions end. This keeps the energy of the audience high as you close your presentation.

- Lisa Ford, CPAE
Author of *How to Give Exceptional Customer Service*

Tip #80. Learn how to perform! My piano teacher once told me that I had to perform, meaning that if the right note was G and I accidentally hit F-sharp, what came after the F-sharp had to sound like I meant to hit F-sharp. Likewise, in speaking, if a sentence or a word just pops out of your mouth, you have to make it sound like it was part of your wonderful script.

- Karla Brandau
Past President, National Speakers Assn., Georgia Chapter
Author of *Winning Mental Calisthenics*

Tip #81. Write down the word "ENTHUSIASM." Now underline <u>IASM</u>; it stands for "I am sold myself." If you're not, don't deliver the talk.

- D. J. Harrington
Author of *Giggle's Christmas Lesson*

155

Tip #82. When you first "take the stage," before you start speaking, stand silently for a moment, focus on the audience and allow them to focus on you, as if to say "hello." Also, at the conclusion of your program, rather than looking down, looking away, or leaving the stage, plant yourself center stage, look directly at the audience and acknowledge their applause. Take it all in, as if to say "thank you."

- Greg Vetter
Author of *Shredding the 13 Myths of the Office*

Tip #83. Don't wear your audience out with any one style. Talk fast and slow, and move from heart, to head, to humor. Physically move toward the audience and then away.

- Terry Paulson, Ph.D., CSP, CPAE
Author of *They Shoot Managers Don't They?*

Tip #84. Start "in sync" with the group. If they are in a fast, upbeat mode, start that way. If they are more sedate (often the case), start that way and gradually pick up the pace.

- Terry Brock, CSP
Past President, National Speakers Assn., Georgia Chapter

Tip #85. The moment you begin speaking, your audience will send you signals, communicating their present state of mind. We all love the feeling of taking an audience to heightened levels of excitement, getting them fully engaged in our message and passion. But, in order to do that, you have to start where they are. Begin on their level. Set your pace by the signals you receive. Then, once your relationship is established, your audience will willingly go with you to higher levels of interest and enthusiasm.

- Dan Thurmon, CSP

Tip #86. A conversational tone is easiest for the audience to appreciate. That old saying, "advice not sought is criticism" speaks the truth. Talk *at* your audience and they'll tune you out. Talk *to* the audience and you'll see heads nodding in agreement with your key points.

- Doug Smart, CSP
Author of *TimeSmart*

Tip #87. Start and end on time.

- Eleanor M. Fountain, Ph.D.
Author of *Success Through Assertiveness*

Tip #88. Learning is not a spectator sport! The more you get your audience involved, the more they will learn. People definitely want content, but they want it delivered in an enjoyable manner.

- Edward E. Scannell, CMP, CSP
Past President, National Speakers Association
Co-Author of the *Games Trainers Play* series

Tip #89. If you go blank, don't panic. It happens to everyone. The ideas and words you want are in your brain; you just need to take a moment to find them. So pause for a moment. A little silence never hurt anyone. Forget the audience, forget your anxiety and just concentrate on remembering.

- Nido Qubein, CSP, CPAE
Past President, National Speakers Association
Author of *How to Be a Great Communicator*

Tip #90. A lack of gestures can mean you are thinking too much about how YOU look to the audience, and "Frankly, Scarlett . . ." When you are able to let go of your worries about how great you are going to look to them, and start worrying about how you help, lift, motivate, and change their actions and attitudes, the gestures will fall into place naturally.

- Lilly Walters
Author of *What to Say When You're Dying on the Platform!*

Tip #91. When you move in front of your audience, "surrender to the moment." Your preparation is past. Leave it there, and focus on what is happening right then—what you are saying, how you feel about what you are saying and, most importantly, focus on the people in your audience. Once you surrender, you will communicate your message in a way that may be different from what you planned, but it will be exactly in tune with the present moment.

- Dan Thurmon, CSP

Tip #92. Prior to walking on the platform, think quietly about the privilege and honor you have been given. Remember that the gift of the spoken word is intended for sharing. Give thanks, be grateful.

- Shirley Garrett, Ph.D.
Past President, National Speakers Assn., Georgia Chapter

Tip #93. Most people are shy about asking the first question; therefore, you may get stymied by an awkward silence. Break the ice by stating the problem and then saying, "Okay, we'll start with the second question!"

- Harvey Mackay, CPAE
Author of NY Times Bestseller
Dig Your Well Before You're Thirsty

*Think as wise men do, but speak
as the common people do.*

Aristotle

Top Professional Speakers'
Secrets for
Using Humor

Tip #94. People remember and laugh more in brightness. Turn the lights up full blast, unless you are showing slides. Then, dim the screen area but light up the audience.

- Harvey Mackay, CPAE
Author of New York Times Best Seller
Dig Your Well Before You're Thirsty

Tip #95. The effectiveness of humor with a point and a purpose is everything. If you are saying things to get a laugh, but misdirect the audience or send them off in another direction, then you are just going to spend time to bring them back.

- Jim Pelley, CSP
Author of *Notable Quotables*

Tip #96. Use humor to deal with distractions. For example, if someone's digital watch or pager beeps during your presentation, you could say, "It's time to take my pill."

- Scott Friedman, CSP
Past President, Colorado Speakers Association
Author of *Using Humor for a Change*

Tip #97. In developing a "signature" story, one of the best places to start is "A most embarrassing moment . . ."

- Jim Pelley, CSP
Author of *Notable Quotables*

Tip #98. Many speakers use tired jokes or overused material in their presentations. If you are going to use humorous material which you did not create yourself, invest in a professional writer who can feed you excellent topical lines for strategic use in your programs.

- Kurt Kilpatrick, JD, CSP, CPAE
Author of *The Executive Treasury of Humor*

Tip #99. Never announce that you're going to tell a joke or a really funny story. This eliminates the surprise factor and sets you up for an expectation level you cannot reach. Just tell the joke or the story.

- Jeff Justice, CSP
Author of *Jeff Justice's Comedy Workshoppe Joke Book*

Tip #100. If all you have is one funny story, you're better off saving it for the body of your talk rather than opening with it. If you open with it, you give your audience a false expectation that more funny things are coming; this causes listeners to wait for more humor and be disappointed when it doesn't come.

- Ken Futch, CSP
Past President, National Speakers Assn., Georgia Chapter

Tip #101. You can never be too clean. When you speak, imagine the Pope is sitting in the back of the room. If something you say would offend him then there's a very good chance it will upset someone in your audience and that's the person your meeting planner will hear from. My theory is, "When in doubt, leave it out."

- Jeff Justice, CSP
Author of *Jeff Justice's Comedy Workshoppe Joke Book*

Appendix

Organizations You Should Know

David Greenberg's Simply Speaking, Inc.®
Toll-Free 1-888-SPEAK-123 (1-888-773-2512)
www.davidgreenberg.com
Our group workshops, private coaching, books and tapes will help
you deliver presentations that get you the results you need.

Creative Training Techniques
7620 West 78th Street, Minneapolis, MN 55439
800-383-9210
Call to request their latest catalog of tools for presenters.

Jeff Justice's Comedy Workshoppe
P.O. Box 52404, Atlanta, GA 30355
404-262-7406
If you are in the Atlanta area and wish to polish or test your
comedic skills, enroll in his workshop.

Toastmasters International
23182 Arroyo Vista, Rancho Santa Margarita, California 92688
800-993-7732
www.toastmasters.org
Call them for a list of Toastmasters clubs in your area.

National Speakers Association
1500 South Priest Drive, Tempe, Arizona 85281
602-968-2552
www.nsaspeaker.org
Call them to find out where your state chapter meets. You can
learn from some of the best professional speakers.

Recommended Books & Tapes

Death by PowerPoint! 50 Simple Ways to Breathe Life into Any Presentation by David Greenberg, Goldleaf Publications.

Forget Your Title... We're All in Sales! Simple Ways to Sell Your Products, Services, and Yourself CD-ROM by David Greenberg, Goldleaf Publications.

The Simple Way to Prepare and Deliver Presentations - A Video Seminar by David Greenberg, Goldleaf Publications.

Classical Communication for the Contemporary Communicator by Halford Ross Ryan, Mayfield Publishing Company. Teaches readers essential communication devices.

Games Trainers Play by John Newstrom and Edward Scannell, McGraw Hill Book Company. This series of books provides hundreds of fun ideas to involve your audiences.

The Quick & Easy Way to Effective Speaking by Dale Carnegie, Pocket Books. Read any book written by Dale Carnegie.

Speak and Grow Rich! by Dotti Walters, Prentice Hall Publishers. Provides an insider's view of the professional speaking and seminar business.

60 Ways to Get Rich and Stay Rich in the Speaking Business by Larry Winget, Win Publishing.

Index

Books and Tapes by David Greenberg

Forget Your Title, We're All in Sales!
Simple Ways to Sell Your Products,
Services and Yourself

Simply Speaking!
The No-Sweat Way to Prepare and
Deliver Presentations

Death by PowerPoint!
50 Simple Ways to Breathe Life
into Any Presentation

The Simple Way to Prepare and Deliver Presentations

Thank God It's Monday!
Designing a Life You Love Beyond the Weekend

Speeches and Workshops
Offered by David Greenberg

The Simple Way to Deliver Winning Presentations!

The Simple Way to Stellar Sales and Service!

The Simple Way to Thrive in the Midst of Change!

The Simple Way to Build Great Teams!

The Simple Way to Motivate
Different Personality Styles!

For information about David Greenberg's speeches, workshops, coaching services or products or to subscribe to his free *Simply Speaking!*® newsletter call toll-free 1-888-773-2512 or visit www.davidgreenberg.com

About the Author

Having overcome his own fear of public speaking, David Greenberg has achieved the highest-earned designation for excellence in the speaking profession, the *Certified Speaking Professional.* This designation is held by less than 7% of the National Speakers Association's 4000 members.

David serves as president of *Simply Speaking, Inc.*®, an Atlanta-based company which has helped more than one hundred thousand people worldwide master the art of effective communication.

For information about David Greenberg's speeches, workshops, coaching services or products or to subscribe to his free *Simply Speaking!*® newsletter call toll-free 1-888-773-2512 or visit www.davidgreenberg.com

CPSIA information can be obtained
at www.ICGtesting.com
Printed in the USA
FSHW010252140919
61993FS